Religious Overreach
at the
Supreme Court

RELIGIOUS OVERREACH
AT THE
SUPREME COURT

SCOTT RUTLEDGE

Algora Publishing
New York

Library of Congress Cataloging-in-Publication Data —

Names: Rutledge, Walter Scott, author.
Title: Religious overreach at the Supreme Court / Scott Rutledge.
Description: New York: Algora Publishing, 2018. | Includes bibliographical
    references.
Identifiers: LCCN 2018035509| ISBN 9781628943603 (soft cover: alk. paper)
    ISBN 9781628943610 (hard cover: alk. paper)
Subjects: LCSH: United States. Supreme Court. | Religion and law—United
    States. | Freedom of religion—United States. | Church and state—United
    States.
Classification: LCC KF8748 .R88 2018 | DDC 342.7308/52—dc23 LC record
available at https://lccn.loc.gov/2018035509

Printed in the United States

It seems to me that the religious instinct is indeed in the process of growing powerfully — but the theistic satisfaction it refuses with deep suspicion.

Friedrich Nietzsche
— *Beyond Good and Evil*

Table of Contents

PREFACE

A failed exorcism: With this description of the Supreme Court's twentieth-century jurisprudence of religion, I might earn some small credit for cleverness. I doubt I will gain much else. And yet, who today can really approve or endorse that tangled body of law?

The Justices of the Court cannot: It provokes more wrangling among them than any other topic. The law professors cannot: They write books attempting to make sense of it, but sense refuses to be made. The citizens supposed to live by it cannot: Nothing incites among them more bitter disagreements.

No, the demons of religious strife have not been banished from our public life by the Court's earnest and repeated exhortations. On the contrary, those fractious spirits are growing bolder and more numerous. And the role of peacemaker in this situation, already tainted by an air of presumptuousness, may also afflict its aspirant with a sense of guilt. He may, despite the best of intentions, be acting as a false prophet. There may be no real peace to be found amidst the clash of religious convictions and passions. Those convictions and passions are many and various, powerful and subtle. They are often most vehement when they are least self-conscious. The best we can do may be to frustrate and confine them, thereby opening up some spaces for civic order and amity.

An American facing this challenge, however, can invoke political memories not easily accessible to other peoples. The statesmen who created the American Republic were historically sophisticated. Their collective learning and experience inspired them to a perspective nearly adequate to the religious challenge — nearly, I say, because the truce they negotiated lasted about a century and a half. There were a few interruptions. There was one massive interruption called the Civil War. But peace was more the rule than the exception, throughout that early period.

Today, however, most citizens of the United States, some sitting on the Supreme Court, have quite forgotten the terms of their nation's original religious settlement. Today the founders' truce is rapidly unravelling. Americans need to relearn the *modus vivendi* of 1787. Year by year, they are more in need of its strategies for the moderation of religious conflict.

This little book is an attempt to assist and promote that relearning.

Chapter 1: Love on Trial

When did the Supreme Court of the United States begin to act as a religious authority? How did it do so?

Above all, why did it do so?

What strange questions, what puzzling questions, for an American to have to ask! And even for those ready to ask them, hindsight may provide only blurred images.

It is not difficult, however, to say when the inquiry took on a new urgency. That occurred in 2015, when the Court told Americans that they had to accept a new way of thinking about marriage. In that year, not content to permit the various state electorates to reconsider and debate their marriage laws, the Court dictated the out-come of those deliberations, in advance, throughout the nation.[*]

In this ruling, the Justices turned their judicial robes into vestments, and themselves into priests.

But perhaps the reader finds these thoughts simply too strange, too unsettling. If so, a moment's reflection

---

[*] Obergefell v. Hodges, 576 U.S. ____ (2015); Docket No. 14-556

upon the meaning of marriage should help.

Whatever else a marriage ceremony may mean, it surely is a celebration of love, a commitment to love, and a consecration of love. Love is one of the mightiest forces moving human beings. Love softens and civilizes that other primal and perennial human motive, hatred. To teach love, to instruct others in loving well, truly, and creatively, is to become a minister to souls and a founder of communities.

Who placed so momentous an authority — evaluating the ways and forms of love, prescribing the liturgies of love — in the nation's judiciary?

Is this a fit role for a few lawyers to take upon themselves?

The five Justices who concurred in the ruling went through some of the motions of grounding their decision in the Constitution. Perhaps they persuaded themselves. It is hard to think that they persuaded anyone who studies that text, or who has any sense of the constitutional history of the Republic. Faced with the vehement objections of four dissenters to the Court's usurpation of legislative prerogatives, the majority responded with speculations about sexual and familial psychology.

But let us defer the constitutional issue for now. Here let us simply note that five Justices employed some very unconstitutional rhetoric in their efforts to convince Americans of the wisdom and propriety of a novel understanding of matrimony. They spoke of the heartfelt anguish of individual litigants. They accused generations of their fellow citizens of cruelty. They waved aside questions about the Court's wisdom for reform, and its calling to reform. They condemned an ancient and long-unquestioned tradition as prejudice and callousness.

In effect, five Justices summoned their fellow citizens to a new exertion of grace and charity. It did not seem to occur to them that those great ideals, so highly charged with subtlety, and ambiguity, and emotion, are virtues central to the world's major religions.

In all this, surely, five Justices revealed a good deal about themselves. Five Justices, in this ruling, proved themselves faithful adherents to a new vision of reality.

Reality! Who dares argue in favor of illusions, and against what is real?

But then, when were true believers, modern or ancient, not convinced that they, at long last, had pierced the veils of appearance and looked upon the very face of truth?

Five Justices spent their best efforts not in probing the logic of the Constitution, but in preaching a sermon. The Court's marriage ruling of 2015 was a religious ruling.

Deeds so startling do not come out of nowhere. They require preparation.

In retrospect, then: What were the earliest omens of the Court's proselytizing?

Let us step back, back through the decades, looking for signs pointing toward this new dispensation, as if we were detectives seeking clues to the unravelling of a mystery. For there is something very surprising here. In a nation whose founders set themselves so firmly against the idea of a national confession, a nation whose citizens long looked askance at official orthodoxies, we should wonder: By what arts or stratagems did the Court come to claim a magisterial and ultimate authority over the most intimate, most sacred of human relations? How widely, and how firmly, is that claim now accepted?

CHAPTER 2: LOGIC ON TRIAL

The best American golfers had become entrepreneurs by the 1990s. One of them, however, seemingly well on his way to celebrity and wealth, found himself facing a cruel obstacle. He suffered from a degenerative disease which was weakening and deforming his legs. Walking the length of a golf course was becoming steadily more difficult and painful for him; nor was his doing so without risk of further medical complications.

He had finished first at numerous youth tournaments. He had excelled in collegiate competitions and had begun to appear in professional events. But now, in order to compete at the highest level, this young man needed to ride a golf cart from shot to shot.

The rules of tournament play, however, included one which required top competitors to walk the full course.

Faced with the waste of his talents and the ruin of his hopes, he requested a waiver of that rule in his case. His request was denied by the association governing the tournaments; and rather than resigning himself to his fate, he sued.

His lawsuit wound up, surprisingly, in the Supreme

Court of the United States.* There, also surprisingly, the young golfer prevailed. And there the exercising of the judicial mind in 2001, as it worked its way to an adjustment of the rules of golf, provided an illuminating perspective upon the evolving character of the nation's highest tribunal.

Consulted about this conflict, surely most people would acknowledge a simple principle governing athletic competitions. Most would agree that in such a contest, if it is to be a true test of skill and strength rather than a social event, each participant must play by the same rules.

The Supreme Court, however, endorsed a rather different principle. The integrity of a competition can remain uncompromised, said the Justices, even if a rule of play is relaxed or eliminated for one of the participants.

A different principle? Is it going too far to say that the Court announced here a contradictory principle? Are these two ethics of sport logically compatible?

The Justices who made up the Court's majority recognized the problem implicit in their ruling. They did not address it directly, however. Rather, they set themselves the task of analyzing golf. They went in search of the essence of the game. They did not search on the golf course, however, but in their judicial chambers. There they found the essential golfing skill to be shot-making. Walking, they said, and the fatigue that walking can generate over a lengthy course, are incidental to the athletic abilities which are engaged and tested in a tournament.

This being so, said the Justices, no significant advantage is gained by a golfer who is allowed to ride a cart, even when others must walk the course. The contest re-

---

* PGA Tour, Inc. v. Martin, 532 U.S. 661 (2001)

mains even-handed.

Two dissenters pointed out that the majority was bending quite out of shape the terms of the statute cited in support of the ruling. These two also urged leaving to golfers themselves, as experts and aficionados, the job of distinguishing golf's essentials from its incidentals. But they failed to persuade their colleagues.

What are we doing when we reason about essences? Where else might we encounter this type of thinking?

We do not encounter it in the practice of modern science. Physicists do not find it useful to speak of the essence of an atom or of a galaxy. They may endorse propositions which seem, to the uninitiated, incompatible. They may say that light behaves as a wave — and that light also behaves as a particle. If pressed to explain themselves, however, they turn to mathematics and to the phenomena which illustrate the application of their mathematical formulations. Numbers, not words, are their tools.

We do hear about essences, however, in various other settings.

Plato, for example, as he studied the world two and a half millennia ago, argued that the essence of an object is to be found in the idea of it, in what he called its ideal form; not in its flawed and temporary physical manifestation.

The central sacrament of the Catholic Church is one in which wine is said to become the blood, and bread the flesh, of Christ. Not that one should expect to find empirical evidence of these so-surprising changes; rather, the nature or essence of the substances is said to be transformed.

Martin Luther stalwartly insisted that the essence of Christian piety is faith; and that true faith, not the deeds of the believer, points the way to salvation.

Into which of these realms — science? philosophy? religion? — would an inquiry into the essence of the game of golf best fit?

Games are human creations and endeavors. As artifices, they ought to tell us something about the artificer. Sports ought to offer, to the discerning, insights as to what it means to be a human being.

In seeking the essence of the game of golf, were the Justices of the Supreme Court engaging that larger question as well?

This much is clear: In deliberating the case before them, the Justices were having recourse to an ancient style of thought and speech. It would be unfair, it might indeed be wrong, to say that their search for the essence of golf was illogical or unreasonable. It is fair to say that they were reaching toward a higher logic, a meta-logic. The idea of essences helped the Justices in looking beyond a merely formal statement of sporting fairness and in thinking more deeply about the clash of simple principles. The idea of essences helped the Justices shine a new light upon the assumption that athletic competitors ought to abide by identical rules of play. The search for an essence led them to temper the stern ethos of sport with the quality of compassion, or mercy.

More generally, perhaps, a focus upon essences might facilitate our incorporation of contradictions, or seeming contradictions, into our thinking. Such a concern, in legal settings, might persuade us that clear reasoning, from consistent premises, plays a lesser role in the law than many of us have supposed.

But the deeper questions remain.

Does the search for essences, in litigation, remain a legal endeavor?

Does that search transform a legal issue into a philosophical inquiry?

Might those searching be pulled even further, even up into the realm of spiritual reflection and choice?

Chapter 3: Nature on Trial

What is a soldier? A good soldier? How is this way of life best learned? Who can most reasonably aspire to it?

These weighty questions, unlikely candidates for judicial resolution, were nonetheless litigated in the United States in the 1990s. The occasion was a suit brought against a small public college, one which, for a century and a half, had devoted itself to the training and education of citizen-soldiers. The college had begun and continued as an all-male school. It imposed upon its new students the physical stress, the intense personal scrutiny, and the harsh discipline of a boot camp, even as it also faced them with a demanding program of academic and moral instruction. A significant number of the school's graduates had gone on to careers in the armed forces, some of them reaching the very highest ranks and providing exemplary leadership in the nation's wars.

In the early 1990s, the school, in accordance with its historical practice, refused admission to a female applicant. Sued for doing so, its leaders defended their policy successfully in the lower courts.

The nation's highest court, however, reversed the ruling in 1996. The Justices declared that as a tax-supported institution, the college could not exclude women from its military style of education. To do so, they said, was to deny female citizens the equal protection of the laws.*

What is a military for?

It is important not to mince words here. The purpose of an army, or a navy or an air force, under the best of circumstances, is intimidation. A strong army puts fear in a potential foe. A strong army, under wise leadership, can sometimes preserve peace. When circumstances cease to be the best, however, when war threatens, the purpose of a military organization can quickly change. Rather than intimidation, its purpose can quickly become the organized perpetration of lethal violence.

We may wish that this were not so. But it would be idle to pretend that the world need worry no more about armed conflict.

It would be equally idle to deny that there has been, historically, a general if not universal consensus among peoples and nations that warfare is the special calling and responsibility of men.

Why, then, might it be thought that an institution whose central purpose is the training and preparation of soldiers must welcome women into its ranks?

Women, some women, no doubt, can become good soldiers. But that isn't quite the question. We need to ask whether good public policy would allow some settings to exist in which military officers can be trained in the traditional ways. And we need to ask, more broadly, whether armies in which both men and women serve in all ranks, and perform all functions, will fight as effectively as their fierce predecessors to be found through-

---

* United States v. Virginia, 518 U.S. 515 (1996)

out the pages of history.

We need to ask these questions — and, we need to recognize that no one knows the answers.

Yet the Court appeared to answer them in 1996.

Were the Justices asserting, or assuming, that our forebears, ancient and modern, have simply erred in their judgment about the nature and the demands of war? That the heavy armor and stout swords of Greek hoplites at Marathon could have been wielded equally well by both sexes? That Roman legions of mixed gender, facing Hannibal, would have fought just as effectively?

These would seem to be very bold assertions indeed.

Or, perhaps, the Justices were thinking that warfare has changed essentially: that violence can now be perpetrated from computer terminals so effectively, and on such a scale, that no one need ever again endure the terrors and the agonies of a battlefield.

This too would seem to be a dubious proposition.

Endorsing any of these ideas, it seems, must involve a rethinking and a reassessment of the human condition.

Human beings, of course, are a part of nature in the large, a part of the whole. And biology, one of nature's voices, has always seemed, to many, to offer a comment or two here.

For one thing, the average young man is taller and heavier and stronger than his average female counterpart. Such differences have never been thought irrelevant to the soldier's life.

For another: To anyone who has dealt with young children and adolescents, it will hardly come as news that the predilection toward physical aggression is not evenly distributed between the sexes.

It is telling in this regard that there is no clamoring, even today, for the integration of athletic competitions. There seems to be no constituency here for man versus woman or for mixed group versus mixed group. Sport is a civilized and regulated facsimile of real struggles, especially of that primal and ultimate struggle, combat. Without the segregation of sports by sex, it might quickly become apparent just how important physical differences can be at the extremes of human endeavor. Mixed-gender sports might quickly make us question whether general integration, one league for all, while it might possibly be fair to a few exceptional women, would be fair to all. We might quickly come to doubt that equal opportunity for males and females in sports is really equal protection.

Might there be good reasons, then, why men have long monopolized the central and the most dangerous military responsibilities?

These are very large questions. Upon the answers can turn the gravest of consequences, for innumerable persons, in unforeseeable circumstances.

The Justices of the Supreme Court did not speak in these terms in 1996. They did not ask what a military is for. They did not really engage the question whether women might be less suited to military endeavors or whether a mixed soldiery might suffer certain handicaps. They concerned themselves with the broad abstractions of the Constitution and with the verbal formulas which lawyers have invented to use in applying those abstractions. They avoided, or they missed, the troublesome assumptions implicit in their ruling and in its possible consequences.

Did the Justices rule well? Did they read the U.S. Constitution truly, in concluding that it requires the correction of a long-standing error about the military?

Again, let us defer the constitutional question. History, in the form of the next war, may provide answers to the practical questions. But litigation before the bar of history, so to speak, may be very costly indeed.

For now, let us merely note that in promoting this identity and interchangeability of males and females, the Justices were engaged in reassessing nature's allocation of gifts, and burdens, between men and women. They were proclaiming a new understanding of the human condition.

CHAPTER 4: PERSECUTION ON TRIAL

Beginning sometime in the 1980s, attentive citizens
of Colorado took notice of a legal innovation occurring
in their midst. Several of the State's cities, and one of
the State's universities, were creating legal protections
— some called them legal privileges — in favor of homosexuals. Under these ordinances and regulations, a
homosexual could bring suit against persons and organizations alleged to have declined various forms of association with him. Controversy arose and spread; and in
1992, a citizens' group managed to put before the voters
a referendum amending Colorado's constitution to nul-
lify and prohibit these new laws.

The voters agreed. A majority did not consider such
measures an advance in civil liberties.

Litigation began promptly in the courts of Colorado.
When it concluded, the State's highest court had ruled
that the constitutional amendment, although unim-
peachable under Colorado law, violated the Constitution of the United States.

The Attorney General of Colorado, however, argued
that the verdict of the referendum was a political deci-

sion properly made by the Colorado electorate. He appealed to the highest court of the nation; but he returned
home, in 1996, with a ruling to the contrary.

And why was the referendum struck down?

Because, said six Justices of the Supreme Court, its
prohibitions were so broad, so harmful, and so difficult
to repeal, that its supporters could only have been motivated by an irrational hostility toward homosexuals.*

There was irony here. This story had begun with an
attempt to de-escalate the tensions between small mi-
norities of homosexuals and the communities in which
they lived. Like many other states, Colorado had long expressed its citizenry's strong disapproval of homosexual
behavior by means of provisions in its penal code. That
is to say that, for a long time, if homosexual Coloradoans
grew careless or indiscreet they risked and sometimes
suffered legal persecution.

Then, in 1971, the Colorado legislature had repealed
the pertinent sections of the State's criminal code.

The repeal could not, of course, change all minds and
soften everyone's behavior overnight. The end of persecution could not immediately erase a history of conflict.
Many Coloradoans would continue to express their convictions on the matter. Friction between the minority
and majority would necessarily continue for some time.

Nor could the end of persecution swiftly assuage the
resentments of its victims, resentments long suppressed
and sometimes refreshed by new offenses. Many of those
formerly persecuted might be tempted to seek revenge.
Others might consider the stigma they had suffered so
unjust as to require bolder public redress. All had a decision to make. They could attack the offensive behavior
they still encountered with a movement of counter-of-
fense. They could organize boycotts of businesses. They

---

* Romer v. Evans, 517 U.S. 620 (1996)

could call upon a sympathetic press to publicize the more colorful incidents. They could make persuasion their policy, and shame their weapon of choice.

Alternatively, they could up the ante. They could seek the satisfaction of persecuting the former persecutors.

Colorado homosexuals chose the latter. Nor did they fail to obtain, from some local authorities if not from the State itself, the right to file lawsuits against their antagonists.

The law speaks, in general, with one of two voices. Civil remedies, such as fines and liens and injunctions, are less intimidating than criminal penalties. The civil suit, however — if widely available and easily invoked — can alter the balance of power in a cultural struggle. A legal change can put on the defensive those formerly able to freely speak their minds and order their affairs. The costs of litigation, even aside from court-imposed sanctions, can push individuals or businesses toward insolvency.

The desire on the part of a badly-treated minority to reciprocate in kind is surely understandable. The results, however, can be unfortunate. In Colorado in 1992 the result of the local ordinances in favor of homosexuals was unfortunate — the counterstroke, the referendum, a blunt and comprehensive legal attack. A majority of Colorado voters tried to stop the newly emerging form of persecution, or of counter-persecution if you will; and to keep the continuing arguments about sexual morality within the realm of persuasion and negotiation.

But the cycle of escalation and counter-escalation, once begun, is not easy to stop. The local struggle, as so often occurred in the United States of the twentieth century, would be merely a prelude to the final escalation, the removal of the issues from the courts of Colorado to the courts of the nation.

At the lower levels of conflict, American law once played a rather modest role. Not that avoidance and shunning were never formalized and enforced by legislators and police and judges. They were — most notably in the matter of race. But avoidance and shunning, across the broad spectrum of social antagonisms in the United States, generally remained just that.

Whatever one's assessment of this history, it is important to recognize that the resort to legal proceedings and sanctions, whatever the justification, raises the stakes. Avoidance ceases to be mere avoidance, shunning becomes more than mere shunning. Those involved become adversaries in a new sense. They may be summoned to court. They must respond there, formally, to the complaints and accusations made against them. If things go badly for them they may be coerced — with a loss of money or property, perhaps even with some loss of their personal freedom. Arguments aimed at moral persuasion are replaced by arguments phrased in the terminology of rights. Each contender is tempted to push his own claim to extremes, and to blacken the conduct and character and motives of his opponent. Efforts directed toward compromise are frustrated. In this environment persons of febrile temperament will often look for trouble; sometimes they will even create trouble where there was none; and they tend to become crusaders.

Nor do the consequences stop with individuals. Very fallible governmental officials must try to distinguish defensible behavior from malice in often ambiguous situations. Supposed wrongdoers must be corrected — too often out of all proportion to the offense. When officials err, the resentments they create are broadcast far and wide. Government risks becoming a cannon aimed at sparrows, provoking the hostility and forfeiting the trust of many of its citizens.

When the resort to litigation is facilitated and encouraged, the courts may become agents of intimidation. A lesson may be widely learned that forthrightness is risky.

The termination of an old persecution is an exercise in soul-shaping. So is the initiation of a new one. Either one changes the character of a society. If such decisions are made by a few rather than by the many, the life of a republic, in which the laws are supposed to be enacted through open deliberation and orderly consensus, is degraded.

When in 1996 the Supreme Court of the United States struck down this Colorado referendum, the Court expanded its supervision of shunning and avoidance to a wide new range of controversies. The Court served notice upon numerous local authorities, who had previously governed these concerns, that they would do so in the future under the watchful eye of the Justices, if at all. A majority of the Justices invited those engaged in an age-old form of religious conflict to persevere all the way to the highest court in the land.

Was this remarkable action required by the Constitution of the United States?

Six Justices argued that it was.

But again, let us defer that question for the present. Let us ask, rather: If those engaged in soulcraft avoid religious terminology and find some other way to explain themselves, does this change the character of their actions?

Chapter 5: Conscience on Trial

In 1983, the Supreme Court pondered the meaning of a provision of the nation's tax code, one which had been the subject of litigation since 1970.* Few taxpayer complaints, perhaps, reach down into the deepest moral strata. This case did. This case was no ordinary wrangling over money.

The controversy had begun when the nation's tax collector, the Internal Revenue Service, changed its interpretation of a statute of long standing. Under that enactment, educational institutions of all kinds had been routinely granted various exemptions which lightened their financial burdens and enabled them to raise funds more easily. Pursuant to a new regulation, however, the IRS notified a few schools that they would no longer enjoy those privileges; and one of them responded with a suit seeking the restoration of its accustomed tax status.

The college in question, regarded by many as retrograde and obstinate, had surely become something of an oddity in its time. As U.S. public opinion was undergoing a fundamental change, its leaders had lagged

---

* Bob Jones University v. United States, 461 U.S. 574 (1983)

behind. The Bible, as understood by the Christian sect which ran the school, was not entirely neutral as to the role of race in human affairs. Although students of all races were admitted, there were, on campus, certain limits imposed upon their social interaction. This contrariety, quite provocative when the nation was renewing its commitment to racial equality, could hardly pass unnoticed. The attentions of hostile politicians and civil rights organizations followed.

It took thirteen years for the validity of the IRS's new regulation to be finally resolved: a resolution adverse to the college. That conclusion may have been a just one, on balance. Yet the case posed troublesome questions, even if justice was served.

Why?

Because the religious character of the controversy was impossible to miss. The Government of the United States was engaged in penalizing, if not in suppressing, the exercise of religious convictions.

The Justices, all of them, much to their credit, were forthright about the religious significance of the case. Both the majority and the lone dissenter agreed that Congress, in granting financial privileges to educational and other charitable organizations, has enough latitude in doing so to further vitally important public policies. Sufficient latitude, indeed, to discourage some religiously motivated conduct.

So far, so good. Racial equality in education had certainly, by this time, become a clear and compelling national policy. The case report could have been ever so short and simple — if Congress had actually written anything about racial equality into the tax exemption statute at issue.

Congress, however, had never done so. Congressmen had discussed doing so, and some had introduced bills for that purpose. But Congress had not changed the existing law.

Where, then, did the IRS get its authority to revise a long-settled interpretation of the law?

The dissenter was clear. The IRS, he said, had no such authority; and the 1970 change, an initiative upon the authority of administrators only, should be struck down. If Congress intended to penalize the college, then Congress could act. Until that occurred, he said, the college should receive equal tax treatment.

Eight Justices, however, disagreed with him. Eight Justices said that there was a proper foundation in the intentions of Congress for what the IRS had done.

Imagine the ambiguity of a mass of evidence concerning the thoughts of hundreds of politicians, about a very divisive issue, over a decade and more.

Congressmen, many of them, probably most of them by the 1970s, would have agreed that racial discrimination, of any kind, in an educational setting, is wrong. Probably few Americans, by that time, would have disagreed. That is not what Congressmen were asked, however.

Congressmen were asked whether they should impose an onerous disadvantage in fundraising upon a small private college which did disagree.

Many Congressmen might have wanted to ponder the second question a bit more. Many a Congressman might have balked. There was, after all, the ideal and the principle of religious liberty to consider. A simple condemnation of racial discrimination need involve no more than aspiration and persuasion. Coupled with a call to action, however — to coercive action against peaceable and law-abiding individuals — that high ideal will seem tainted in the eyes of many. Aspiration and persuasion do not sit comfortably, for many, alongside aggressive intolerance.

Is a refusal to be racially color-blind, in any and all settings, sufficient justification for placing a class of citizens of the United States into a legally disfavored status? Did Congress really intend, as a legislative body, that those who, for religious reasons, still observed some racial distinctions, be put at a financial disadvantage in educating their young?

Since 1970 the nation's legislators had hesitated; and there the matter sat until 1983, when eight Justices decided that in the absence of suitable legislative action, they would ascertain and declare the intent of Congress.

It is the very business of legislators, representing a cross-section of the larger community, to deliberate troubling and contentious issues in search of a consensus of judgment and conscience. Upon finding that consensus, it is their duty to formalize and declare it.

And upon failing to find it? Shouldn't they then refrain from acting?

Uncomfortable, perhaps, with their judicial shortcut to a legislative consensus, the Justices raised their sights. Going over the heads of Congressmen, they appealed to the conscience of the nation. For the college to merit its tax privileges, said the Justices, "The institution's purpose must not be so at odds with the common community conscience as to undermine any public benefit that might otherwise be conferred."

It is unlikely that the Justices were misreading the common community conscience on the general topic of racial discrimination. It is clear, however, that the Justices were oversimplifying. The beleaguered college was pleading for its liberty, its religious liberty. Are we to believe that only a few Americans would have granted that plea any urgency? Was the common community conscience — if we may speak so — simply unequal to such a challenge? Or would many Americans, citizens of a nation dedicated to the ideal of religious liberty, have sought creative ways, possibly new ways, to accommodate religious liberty to the demand for racial equality?

The American conscience, represented in Congress no less than in the Supreme Court, was engaged in deliberating the problem. But the tension could hardly have been clarified so sharply, or so suddenly, in the public mind.

Who can see into the mind of another? Who can disentangle, without fail, the various, often subtle, and sometimes conflicting thoughts which go into a judgment of conscience — even into one's own judgment of conscience, let alone someone else's?

Who, then, confidently reads the consciences of a shifting cast of four or five hundred Senators and Representatives, as they come and go, playing the game of politics, over years, even decades? Who will claim sufficient clairvoyance to speak for several hundred millions, where even an assembly of modest size finds itself divided?

Did the American conscience, in all the fullness of its experience, in all the ambiguity of its many ideals, really have no room in 1983 for a small school, on private property and among voluntary associations, at the margins of vast educational establishment, to behave offensively?

No, answered the Court.

The Court's answer, admittedly, represented a consensus among more than just eight individuals and a few administrators. It probably represented the convictions and the passions of millions of Americans. Nonetheless, reading a vast nation's mind remains a formidable endeavor.

And what about the eight individual consciences

who announced that reading?

The Justices did not reflect, in print, upon their own backgrounds and perspectives. It would have been unseemly for them to do so in a judicial opinion. We as readers, however, can hardly help noticing the extraordinary nature of this task they assigned themselves. We can hardly help wondering about their fitness for such a challenge.

Didn't those very few consciences, in order to preside impartially, need to take up the stance of all the participants in the controversy? Didn't they need to sift the consciences of others, measure the consciences of others, weigh and balance the consciences of others — maintaining all the while their independence?

To assess adequately the consciences of several hundred million persons would seem to require moral omniscience.

To sum up accurately all the ambiguous and even conflicting ethical judgments of several hundred million persons, would seem to require moral infallibility.

These few Justices, by invoking the nation's conscience, called upon themselves to become universal consciences — to understand, and to put in well-reasoned order all the diverse judgments and emotions which continually agitate human beings.

A universal conscience! The very idea has theological resonance.

Thus did the Justices, once again, venture into a realm of religious reasoning.

CHAPTER 6: NATIVITY ON TRIAL

Liberation narratives are woven into the fabric of American experience.

Think of those sturdy Puritans of the 1600s, braving stormy seas and harsh New England winters to found their shining city on a hill.

Think of the War of Independence beginning in the 1770s, waged against the English King and aristocracy.

Think of the frontiers to the west, steadily receding but long irresistible to those undaunted by the dangers and hardships.

Think of the long struggle against slavery, and then the Civil War.

Think of the Mormons fleeing the hostility of their neighbors across the continent to an arid and sparsely populated land.

Think of the nineteenth and early twentieth century crusade to liberate Americans from the evils of intoxicating liquors, culminating in the enactment of a constitutional amendment in 1919 (and then the counter-liberation, its repeal, after only fourteen years).

Think of the many individuals and organizations

who strove in the twentieth century to make good the promise of civic equality which earlier generations could not fulfill.

Think of the countless persons and groups who have woven in and around these epics their own stories of moving and searching and building anew.

Not so long ago, most Americans learned their Exodus early and well. Many today have the spirit of that book in their bones. Many, that is to say, are more than merely receptive to the idea of a new liberation.

It should not be surprising, then, that scientific and medical advances, some of them pioneered in the United States, suggested to not a few Americans a modern frontier: a way hitherto little traveled, but rich, perhaps, in unimagined possibilities.

This new promised land, its would-be inhabitants discernible even in the nineteenth century, began to beckon widely and strongly by the twentieth: a realm in which women, in approaching the fundamental choices which shape their lives, encounter no obstacles due to their sex.

Surely some women, always, must have chafed under the risks and the burdens of pregnancy and motherhood. Few had ever avoided those risks and burdens. Few, if they questioned at all, failed to resign themselves to a limitation of their choices. In the twentieth century, however, what few had imagined, and even fewer managed, became a real possibility. With pregnancy an option to be chosen, and universally known to be so, an ancient grievance felt by some could be fanned into the flames of a widespread and open rebellion. Now what we might call feminine declarations of independence — of each woman's right to free herself from the constraints that biology had always imposed — became common. Now more and more women sought to move out into the wider world, upon a basis of equality with men, into fields of endeavor in which their sex had seldom been seen.

New and reasonably effective methods of contraception invited women to join this hopeful march into the future. But the invitation carried no guarantee. Contraception can fail, even when used properly. It can be forgotten or misapplied. Its use can be attended by complications. It offers a mitigation, not an elimination, of the special concerns with which the daughters of Eve have always contended.

Medically competent abortion procedures, therefore, another modern development, came to appear, to many, as an urgent emancipation — as the means by which to realize that comprehensive freedom, at last, which contraception promised but could not quite deliver. With this additional assistance, an accidental conception could be terminated even after the fact. With this, a woman need never carry a pregnancy to term, or assume an unwanted parental responsibility.

One large obstacle, however, still stood in the way. A great many people, indeed majorities in various electorates, regarded abortion as an act which, if not strictly infanticide, was very similar to it. Many American states restricted the procedure to narrow circumstances, and an abortionist or his patient could be prosecuted for stretching or ignoring those limits.

By the mid-twentieth century, however, legislatures in a number of American states had begun to allow pregnancies to be medically terminated under some circumstances. Debate was proceeding, at different paces and with varying results, from state to state and region to region.

The debates were proceeding too indecisively, however, for some of the most earnest participants — too slowly for some, too rapidly for others.

Into this contested but not disorderly situation stepped the United States Supreme Court in 1973, with a pair of linked decisions which effectively nullified local abortion restrictions throughout the United States.* And thereupon began an agitation and a rancor which have continued, with no end in sight.

It is easy to see the concerns felt by those who condemn the Court's initiative. What has always struck so many people about abortion, and what strikes them today, is the destruction of a life-in-becoming, a human life-in-becoming.

Nor need we puzzle over the allure of abortion-on-demand to many women. For it seemed to offer a freedom of action which their forebears, stretching back through the generations time out of mind, could hardly have dreamt.

Apparent also, however, are the large and troublesome questions posed by the Court's action.

Just how similar are abortion and infanticide? Are they kindred assaults upon a human being? If so, does the good to be found in abortion-on-demand outweigh the evil in it? Is it good for the woman who takes advantage of it? For the community in which she lives?

Or might there be, on balance, more harm than good in it?

No one has found a way to calm these troubled waters. Perhaps there is no calming them. Perhaps the meaning and the importance of nativity reach too deep into the human soul for easy answers.

What would the American law of abortion look like today, if the dissenting Justices had persuaded their

---

* Roe v. Wade, 410 U.S. 113 (1973); Doe v. Bolton, 410 U.S. 179 (1973)

brethren in 1973?

We may be certain that fifty state legislatures, and fifty state judiciaries, working independently, would not have converged upon one policy. Some might have followed the path taken by the Supreme Court. Some might have retained much of their earlier law on the topic. Some might have found yet different approaches.

We may be certain, that is, that the promptings of conscience, as given expression by many thousands of local legislators and judges, would have been complex and diverse. We may be certain that those statutes and court rulings would have reflected the variety of opinion to be found among many millions of citizens.

Do some deny that abortion is an issue of conscience? They should be a minority; for if the decision to cut short a budding young life isn't disturbing, what would be?

Viewed in this light, in the light of conscience, the Justices' ruling is an especially interesting one. For implicit in that ruling is one of two assertions.

Were the Justices, perhaps, denying that there is such a thing as a collective or communal conscience? Were they insisting that conscience is strictly an individual phenomenon, lacking any commonality which might unite numerous consciences in a legitimate consensus? But we have just seen how, in 1983, the Justices, a number of them the same as in 1973, rested a very sensitive ruling upon what they called the "common community conscience." Let us offer them the respect, then, of assuming that they would not so blatantly contradict themselves within one decade.

Perhaps, then, the Justices were asserting that the conscience of the community, the collective conscience, if adverse to abortion, is transparently unjust. Perhaps, acknowledging the existence of a common community conscience here, they overruled its judgment in the name of a higher conscience — in the name of a universal conscience, so to speak.

But how did the Justices assure themselves of their unobstructed access to the promptings of that higher or universal conscience? Whence their certainty that the nation's incontrovertible moral duty requires the elimination of any real limits upon the practice of abortion?

The Justices did not dwell upon the meaning of conscience, however, or upon logical problems, in 1973. Perhaps this is not surprising. Such inquiries might not have proven helpful to them. And there were other lines of inquiry they did not pursue.

Does the free and common practice of abortion promote human flourishing? Is this way of life in harmony with human nature? Might there be an ecology, so to speak, of human procreation? A balance, and an order, which we might not fully understand?

To put it a little differently: Was nature being capricious in sundering humanity right down the center? In denying half the species the pleasures of a worry-free dalliance with the other sex? In burdening that half so heavily with the consequences of the act of mating, and forcing them to put so much more thought and care into profound and life-shaping decisions about courtship and parenthood? Whether capricious or purposeful, has nature sewn into woman, over long ages, a distinctive approach to these concerns?

Have traditional cultures cunningly reinforced nature with what amounts to a disguised matriarchy? Have men, under a conceit of dominance, long been drawn into the service of their women and children?

What about the implications here for children? For parents? For the formation and flourishing of families? For the well-being of future generations?

The Justices of 1973 discussed none of this. That does not mean, however, that their ruling had no bearing upon such vital questions. In putting nativity on trial, the Court actually took on much more. The Court declared itself a staunch advocate of change in the age-old ways of reproduction and renewal. Seven Justices put nature herself on trial — as they would again in 1996.

Nor is it likely to have escaped the reader that questions about love, about how, and whom, and when to love, cannot be separated from questions about nativity. Love is one of the fundamental forces which create and sustain human communities. Love makes persons out of physical organisms. Love redeems lives which might otherwise merit the famous description: solitary, poor, nasty, brutish, and short. Those who teach love are poets, and ultimately legislators.

How did Eros and Aphrodite fare in the Supreme Court? Were these Greek gods infused with new vigor by the loosing of their ties to procreation? Or did they find themselves weakened and disoriented? More generally: Agape is the Greek term for a general beneficence toward others, a real interest in their well-being. Was this desirable character nourished in 1973? Or might it have been subtly poisoned? How does one generation act lovingly toward its posterity? When does the microscopic being which, uninterrupted, will become human, make that transition? When should a life-in-becoming be nourished and protected by the human community which it might enlarge and enrich?

And why, finally, were these profound and troublesome questions thought to be judicial in character?

The Justices insisted, as is the wont of Justices, that they were merely interpreting the Constitution. Here, however, the scholarly consensus is sharply adverse. Even among those pleased by the new law of abortion, few have taken seriously the Court's efforts to demonstrate that law's constitutional provenance.

Again, however, let us defer that issue. Let us simply note that here we see the Court fully engaged in a religious calling: shaping not just the souls, but the bodies also, of coming generations.

CHAPTER 7: SEXUALITY ON TRIAL

In the 1960s, the State of Connecticut still had on its statute books a nineteenth-century enactment which threatened users of contraceptive devices with a fine or with imprisonment up to a year. It appears, however, that those penalties had long been honored with neglect rather than enforcement, and that by the middle of the twentieth century, if not earlier, no prosecutions were being brought under the old law.

One Connecticut prosecutor, however, coupling the prohibition with a separate statute punishing the offense of assisting another in the commission of a crime, did bring charges against an executive and a physician who operated a clinic offering birth control information and supplies. The accused were convicted as accessories, and fined $100 each. When the Connecticut courts denied their appeals, they turned to the United States Supreme Court; and there, in 1965, their convictions, along with the antiquated contraceptive ban, were annulled.*

The decision was not a close one. Six Justices made up the majority while two dissented. However the

---

* Griswold v. Connecticut, 381 U.S. 479 (1965)

Court's opinion was curiously splintered, featuring no fewer than four different attempts to explain the ruling. And the Justices' unusual eagerness to express themselves was only one oddity among several.

In fact the oddities of this case invite, and very richly reward, a careful review.

Oddity: The majority Justices resorted to a good deal of rummaging about in search of a legal basis for their decision. Before they were done, no fewer than six different provisions of the Constitution had been called upon. None of those provisions, however, said anything about sexual morality or sexual behavior.

Three Justices, provoking a little diplomatic scoffing from one of their colleagues, even insisted upon the importance of the Ninth Amendment — an affirmation of the rights of the people so very abstract that it is hardly ever cited by the Court.

On vivid display, then, were both the Justices' difficulties in finding some way to make the spare language of the Constitution seem to yield the ruling they wanted, and their determination to do so.

Oddity: Finding nothing really helpful in the Constitution, the Justices turned to their own ideas and concerns and experiences. They spoke of privacy and of the importance of privacy to husbands and wives.

But no one's privacy was actually at issue in the case. The State of Connecticut had brought no one into court to answer a charge of using contraception; although surely many couples there, many indeed by the 1960s, were doing so. Apparently no prosecutor considered pressing charges like that a good career move. The old law had become symbolic in character, an expression of judgments once, but no longer, widely shared.

To the defendants actually in court, of course — sum-

moned for the public act of making contraceptive devices widely available — the case was no mere exercise in
litigation as a form of theater. The legal condemnation
of their stock in trade was more than an annoyance. Although they could probably have handled an occasional modest fine as a cost of providing their service, few
people would choose to be the subject of a criminal proceeding or to risk the consequences of conviction just to
make a statement of principle.

And yet — a further oddity — if we try to make the
harassment of birth control clinics a convincing rationale for the Court's intervention, the Justices themselves bring us up short. For several of them affirmed,
and none disputed, the authority of the State of Connecticut to regulate or even prohibit the offending commerce, should its legislature choose to do so.

An oddity of omission: History, surely on trial here,
makes no appearance in the case.

The contraception law at issue was about a century
old. Yet no Justice asked why it had been enacted. No
Justice observed that in the nineteenth century, every
Protestant denomination in the United States, as well as
the Catholic Church, condemned and opposed artificial
birth control. No Justice inquired whether the statute
might have been a religiously-motivated attempt, clum-
sily executed, to bring the weight of public opinion to
bear upon sexual practices thought likely to have a del-
eterious effect upon relations between men and women,
and thereby upon later generations.

No Justice, that is, whether voting to strike down
the ban or to leave its future to officials of the State,
seemed to recognize it as religious legislation. A state
government's embodiment of religious purposes in its
laws had, for some decades prior to 1965, been subject
to the Court's review upon that basis alone. The Justices

might easily have made their decision much more co-
herent. Only four years earlier they had deliberated at
length over the legitimacy of a patchwork of commercial
restrictions enforced only upon Sunday, the Christian
Sabbath.*

In the original character of the law they were striking
down, however, none of the Justices seemed interested.
What they all seemed to see in the old statute received
its most pointed expression, ironically, from one of the
dissenters, who prefaced thus his explanation of why its
repeal should be left to the state legislature: "I think that
this is an uncommonly silly law."

A philosophical oddity: Several of the Justices, even as
they presented their constitutional interpretation, said
plainly enough that they really didn't think the effort
necessary. Three of them told their readers, in effect, not
to worry about the text-reading, the precedent-citing,
the logic-chopping. They were looking for their authority to something older than the Constitution, something
higher than the Constitution.

Three of the Justices, that is to say, invoked the ancient concept of a law of nature.

Is it possible that nature's assessment of the practice
of contraception might be a little unclear? No matter.
Nature's assessment of attempts to forbid contraception, for three of the Justices, was not unclear.

But invocations of the laws of nature, common
enough in an earlier era of American jurisprudence, had
gone quite out of style by the twentieth century. The
Justices' resort to this older school of legal reasoning
strongly suggested that something very unusual was going on.

By 1965 a great many people, in the United States and

---

* McGowan v. Maryland, 366 U.S. 420 (1961)

elsewhere, were unable or unwilling to see contraception as anything but a pure liberation, a technical advance without any undesirable side effects or unforeseen consequences. The Justices, apparently, fully agreed. To them the Connecticut case seemed an inexplicably aggressive intervention by public officials in matters quite definitely, even incontrovertibly, none of the public's business. And it is in the Justices' myopia, or their reticence, that we can find a clue as to the subtext causing them to expend such large efforts to so little purpose in trying to explain themselves. The case, at least in part, was about the very sensitive topic of sexual morality.

The case was also about privacy, granted; but the privacy of conduct cannot be assessed without reference to its possible public consequences. This conflict raised the question whether the most intimate relations between men and women might be a fit subject for public attention; whether some things might be wholesome, and some not, even in those settings; and whether there might be important public consequences attending the prevailing sexual mores.

Sexual morality, in general, had never been thought within the purview of the Supreme Court of the United States. Sexual morality, in the American scheme of government, had been a concern for state governments, not for the nation's government. Moreover, it had hardly been the view of earlier generations that sexual mores and sexual behavior were individual concerns only, having no public consequences and calling for no public action. To earlier generations, artificial contraception had posed fundamental questions about human sexuality, and therefore about human nature in general.

There can be, of course, no one way to articulate the sexual sensibilities and judgments of a time rapidly receding from memory. Doubtless some of those sensibilities and judgments have become invisible to a great many people today. It is important, however, to try to recognize such concerns and to recover some of the frame of mind which gave rise to them. Here follows an attempt.

Is a sense of gravity, of high stakes — of risks taken and burdens assumed, therefore of caution — natural, or intuitive, to one at least of the two sexes? Might such a sense bear upon the quality of relations between them? How, and to what effect?

Does casual sex pose special risks to women? Does it pose subtler but still serious risks to men? Do banality and boredom threaten when a sense of levity pervades the sexual atmosphere?

Is partnership in parenthood one of the consummations of human experience? Does human nature call both men and women to this endeavor?

And what about children? Do persons yet to be born have an invisible but vital stake in today's cultural proprieties and public policies?

If recreational sex should become widely practiced, what would happen to marriage rates? To the character of a people? Would there be a general shift toward hedonism and away from more demanding ethical standards?

How important are high marriage rates to the long-term health of a society? How important is fecundity to the long-term health of a society?

Does a democratic citizenry have a proper role to play, a public and collective role, in seeking consensus as to what are better and what are worse expressions of sexuality?

How likely is a community's official stance upon these sensitive topics — its preaching, if you will — to improve, or to degrade, behavior?

The baffled heralds of a new sexual dispensation:

Would this description be unfair to the Justices of 1965?

Heralds: Although they were not surprising the avant-garde, nor indeed a sizable segment of their fellow citizens, the Justices were announcing a new age to a great many who still rested in the bosom of tradition.

And if the Justices were heralds, they were baffled in at least two senses. They seemed to show no understanding or even awareness why their news might actually be news to anyone. They no longer seemed conversant with the world of their forebears nor concerned that anyone might question or criticize their hostility to the old statute. They were baffled, also, in struggling with a constitutional text resolutely silent regarding their altered sensibilities and their novel imperatives. They had to work hard and play loose in extracting from that text a new legal mandate.

The Justices were being carried along by the waves of religious change that were sweeping through American society. They did not understand themselves in those terms. They also failed to see that they were doing what jurists, as jurists, are especially supposed to avoid. They were ruling before all the evidence (even worse, before hardly any of the evidence) was in, and without both sides being fairly heard. And in doing so, they were appointing themselves curators of the American soul in a central and crucial dimension of life.

Chapter 8: Imagination on Trial

How is it that a prayer is sometimes found offensive? What is said might be resented. The manner of address might seem inappropriate in some way. Personal styles or interests might clash — not to mention theological convictions. But suppose offense is taken at a deeper level. Suppose the act of praying is found offensive.

Why might that happen?

No matter how generic a prayer has become, no matter how much it mutes the themes and passions of the great monotheisms, still, it is likely to express clearly enough several perspectives or beliefs. Even a god whose felt presence has waned still signifies a universe which is, in some sense, personal. In praying, human minds address themselves to mind-as-such — to Mind, so to speak. One who prays posits mindfulness, rather than inertness or indifference, as an essential feature of reality. He assumes that there are purposes of a higher order. He suggests that the larger world is consciously responsive, in some important if elusive sense, to human fears and hopes and efforts.

The postulation of a hierarchy in the very nature of things has further implications. Prayer also suggests that dependency may be an unavoidable feature of the human condition. Those who pray confess that they may be subject, ultimately, to a power or powers beyond their understanding and control. They acknowledge blessings received. They recognize the possibility of limitations and principles binding upon them, limitations and principles they have not created and to which they have not consented. They admit that all too often, human means are insufficient or human efforts misdirected.

One who speaks a prayer with conviction, therefore, takes up a certain stance toward life. He or she, a sentient part contemplating the unfathomable whole, displays a characteristic demeanor: a receptiveness to mystery, an intimation of higher authority, a reverence and a readiness to serve, and an acknowledgment of neediness.

Piety is a name frequently given to this frame of mind. Its place among the virtues was secure in many cultures, not just among monotheists.

On the other hand, one who objects to prayer, to the act of praying itself, may be displeased, may even be scandalized, by these pious assumptions and attitudes. Perhaps he sees no purpose higher in rank, nor more worthy, than the human will. Perhaps he is convinced that the cosmos is mindless and entirely neutral with regard to mankind. And perhaps he hears, in prayerful expressions of gratitude or supplication, an unhealthy tendency toward superstition, or dependency, or servility.

For some of these reasons, or for all, he who objects to prayer does not consider traditional piety nourishing to the virtues or fortifying to the character.

Prayer came to serve, for some twentieth-century Americans, as a sort of litmus test. Responses tended to sort people into groups, not precisely but roughly: groups in which different readings of human nature and different approaches to human felicity prevailed.

Many felt that a young person who senses an unseen power, mindful and attentive, who turns toward nature, and nature's God, for guidance and assistance, was likely to be helped, not hindered, along the road of life.

For others, that young person would be having his head filled with ideas that are at best false, and quite possibly harmful.

By the mid-twentieth century, these concerns and divisions inevitably generated conflict in educational settings. Some parents of children or adolescents required to listen to a teacher recite a daily prayer felt compelled to object. No one wants a child taught error. No one has an obligation to remain silent while a child is being miseducated. And surely several hundred years of Western philosophy had given such a parent authorities to cite, and arguments to make, against theism.

Thus it was that in 1962, the Supreme Court of the United States addressed itself to the question of official prayers recited in public, tax-supported schools. At the time, teachers and students frequently began their day with a brief ceremonial address to Deity. This had been common from the very inception of governmental systems of education in America. In that year however, six Justices decided that the practice represented an official establishment of religion, and was therefore constitutionally impermissible.[*]

In contemplating the ruling, it is well to keep in mind the short prayer that offended, one composed by a state agency for elementary and secondary schools:

Almighty God, we acknowledge our depen-

---

[*] Engel v. Vitale, 370 U.S. 421 (1962)

dence upon Thee, and we beg Thy blessings upon
us, our parents, our teachers, and our country.

These few words surely represent a modest theism,
we might almost say a vestigial theism. Here we find no
account of creation, no founder or messiah or blessed
one, no narrative of redemption, no vision of the world
to come, no stern moral commandments, no modes of
worship, no mandatory rites or disciplines. The God
on display in this little prayer might almost have with-
drawn from the scene of human affairs.

The prayer that was prohibited, that is, already represented an earnest attempt, made at the lower levels
of American government, to find an acceptable compromise between American theists and American anti-
theists. But compromise held no appeal for six Justices
in 1962.

It is well also to recall the anger which greeted the
ruling. Many Americans considered the Court's decision
a grievous error.

Much discussion, and much argument, ensued. The
discussions and arguments have since abated, but not
stopped. The question of error, unsurprisingly, has usually been central: Did the Justices read the Constitution
correctly? Or did they arbitrarily impose their personal
preferences upon their fellow citizens?

It is useful, however, to approach the controversy
from a different angle. Let us ask: Does prayer tend to
stimulate, or to stunt, the human imagination? Does the
act of addressing a divine being — of positing a living
and responsive cosmos — tend to inspire and liberate a
young mind? Or, might the cultivation of a very different
mental world — one set against a background of ran-
dom and purposeless materiality — point children and

adolescents more reliably to a flourishing life?

But, some will ask, do these two visions, so stark in their contrast, both require an effort of imagination?

Already, among the Greeks and Romans, there were some thinkers who regarded the very idea of deity as an extravagance of human invention, and who charged their contemporaries with gross naivety. A few even tried to explain the world in strictly sensuous and material terms. The early atheists were always a small minority, however. For most people, then and until relatively recent times, theism, in one form or another, set the background against which they lived their lives. Gods and lesser spirits were simply assumed to have important roles to play in the human drama. In those earlier times, it seems, strenuous feats of imagination were required of those who denied, not of those who believed.

Today we frequently hear, however, that the stunning achievements of modern science have reversed this polarity. The burden of proof now, it is argued, rests upon those who doubt that the laws of physics can explain everything. Now we easily imagine, now we do not even need to imagine, a universe in which mind and purpose, the quintessentially human phenomena, are a sort of trick played upon us by nature. Now the ancient illusions can be effectively expunged — and should be. Now theism stands exposed as primitive anthropomorphism and bad science.

Is the matter really so simple? It might be pertinent to recall that the new sciences, arising several centuries ago and eventually transforming whole cultures and environments, were conceived and nurtured by theists. Their religious convictions, apparently, did not inhibit their creativity. The most famous of them, Isaac Newton, put as much effort into theology as he did into his physics and mathematics. And today, it is not hard to find highly-credentialed and respected scientists who, when not in the laboratory, may be seen in a church or a synagogue. The supposed war between science and theism is an idea of relatively recent origin.

But here we may be up against one of those ultimate issues, unresolvable in principle, which eventually defeat those so rash as to assert a final answer. Nor is it impossible that the question posed above, seemingly more modest, is of the same type: Which of the two visions outlined above is more likely to enrich a young imagination?

Be that as it may, when confronted by would-be educators who would direct the schooling of our children, we are entitled to ask some questions. Since six Supreme Court Justices took this authority upon themselves in 1962, surely we are more than entitled, surely we are called upon, to ask: What about the quality and the character of those jurists' imaginations? Do we find there something to emulate, or to criticize?

Why did six Supreme Court Justices, in 1962, consider themselves authorized to require public schools to quarantine, if not prohibit, open expressions of an ancient and traditional understanding of the world?

Because, they said: "The Establishment Clause... stands as an expression of principle on the part of the Founders of our Constitution that religion is too personal, too sacred, too holy to permit its unhallowed perversion by a civil magistrate."

But this will not do. The Justices' language here is much too strong. Where is the evidence that the American founders considered the offering of a prayer by a civil magistrate in a public setting an unhallowed perversion? Generations of Americans had lived with public expressions of piety constantly and comfortably. The commencement of formal and official occasions with a prayer was a venerable American tradition. No group was well met, nor any important business properly begun, but with due ceremonial obeisance. This communal sensibility was not just prevalent, it was widely cultivated, certainly through the nineteenth century and well into the twentieth.

Nor did the Justices do any better with their religious history. The fathers and leading spirits of the great religions, had they been admonished to regard their devotions as personal concerns merely, would have been incredulous, or contemptuous, or both. They and their disciples reached out and taught as widely as they could. They shaped the characters of peoples. They inspired powerful and enduring institutions. They took the greatest care to pass along their convictions and their ethos to new generations. They built religious communities, strong communities whose leaders strove to instill in the faithful the favored beliefs and practices. The occasional individual preaching a private and personal religion might have been tolerated, but was surely an oddity.

Six Justices, in other words, here imagined for themselves a more useful past. In doing so, they got the history of their nation, both civic and religious, wrong. Their error might have recommended to their fellow citizens some misgivings about the Justices' qualifications as guides to the future. It might have suggested that there is danger in making a very few individuals, so limited in knowledge, so prone to bias, tutors to many millions of young minds. It might have advised against the displacement of parents and local communities from a long-accustomed role — that of deciding what vision of the world, or what alternate and competing visions, to present to the young.

In the United States, the question of the proper role of local communities in education is not only prudential, it is also constitutional. But we are deferring this issue for a while.

Chapter 9. Art on Trial

The father of Western philosophy, two and a half millennia ago, offered some reflections upon the nature of beauty, and upon the allure of the beautiful. A character in one of his dialogues, said to be eminently wise, placed beauty's essence in a higher realm of being, a realm of pure forms. She described those abstract forms as eternal, unchanging, and unblemished by the many flaws to be seen in their transient earthly instances or imitations. Beauty, she said, the essence of beauty, was one such form among many; something discernible in each and every beautiful thing.

She argued also that human beings, at their best, could apprehend the true form of beauty. But she emphasized the necessity of a careful and sustained education in and to the beautiful, and away from all that is ugly, or vulgar, or degraded.

Thus began the field of inquiry known as aesthetics.

Since then, of course, many have taken up these questions. A large body of thought has accumulated. The philosophy of beauty has had many distinguished practitioners. Disagreements upon its most fundamental questions persist.

There is no consensus that each instance of beauty reflects an eternal essence of beauty.

Does beauty inhere in what is beautiful, or is it born in the response of a beholder? There is no consensus.

Does reason have a role to play in our judgments about the beautiful? Some say not.

Must we be educated to a sound aesthetic sensibility? Some have argued that the faculty is innate — effortlessly present in one person, inaccessible to another.

There may even be aestheticians today who decline to speak of a sound aesthetic sensibility, or to call any art ugly, or vulgar, or degraded.

Likewise, though there has been much speculation, there is argument over the connection, if any, between aesthetics and broader concerns. Does art, good art, fine art, offer a path leading those who follow it toward what is good in general, and away from what is bad? Does a proper appreciation of beauty teach virtue and elevate behavior? Does it enrich the imagination, or enlarge the understanding?

These last issues are of special concern. For many have thought, many continue to think, that artistic skills can be abused. Many fear that a craftsman's work, if it flatters a vicious or degraded character, if it promotes a deformed imagination or an impaired understanding, can cultivate the vices to which human beings perennially prove themselves all too susceptible.

Especially in the case of children and adolescents, so impressionable, so malleable, many worry that bad art can be a malign and powerful influence.

And hovering in the background, of course, remains the central question: What is good art? What distinguishes bad art?

But even as we ask, we realize that any general agreement upon standards will be stubbornly elusive.

These are deep waters. Well may we be uneasy when we find public officials swimming in them. Yet public officials, monarchs and legislatures and executives and courts, always have. Those charged with governmental responsibilities cannot justify awaiting the resolution of a debate unlikely ever to be resolved. Historically, the reality of bad art has always been assumed — not just art of poor quality, but art which stimulates destructive behavior. Censorship continues, at least to some extent, even today. Some literary and graphic productions have always been targeted for suppression, and their producers or distributors summoned before courts of law.

In the United States, the power to censor long remained principally in the hands of the local governments; although the central government, as the agency charged with delivering the mail, also attempted to police those channels against the most offensive materials. As with so many governmental functions, however, this division of responsibilities began to shift in the twentieth century: the central authorities expanding their reach, the local being displaced.

Thus it was that the Supreme Court of the United States, in 1957, ruled upon two governmental efforts to condemn certain publications as unworthy of legal protection.* One of the proceedings had been originated by a state government; the other by the central or federal government. In the lower courts, both cases had culminated in a judgment of obscenity and a criminal conviction of the publisher. The Court affirmed both rulings. Disagreements among the Justices, however, resulted in four written opinions.

Six Justices endorsed the controlling opinion, al-

---

* Roth v. United States, 354 U.S. 476 (1957)

though one of them wrote separately to express his reservations about doing so.

One Justice split his vote: arguing for affirmation of the state conviction, but for reversal of the federal conviction.

Two Justices, however, called for nothing less than a comprehensive end to censorship — for a prohibition, applying to all American governments, municipal, state, and federal, of any attempt to interfere with literary or graphic expression.

The disagreements, that is to say, reached down into fundamentals. Surely that is not surprising. The best efforts of outstanding aestheticians, for many centuries, have managed to shorten the list of open questions little, if any. How, then, could nine busy judges, pressed for time, trying to get through a docket crowded by controversies many and diverse, hope to speak here with one voice?

From the Court's splintering factions, however, a little more than just confusion can be gleaned.

Only two Justices sought to have American law, at all levels, shut its eyes against bad art. Seven Justices, that day in 1957, committed themselves to the proposition that some art is bad, so bad as to be demoralizing and harmful. Seven declined their colleagues' invitation to issue a universal condemnation of censorship. If these seven failed to offer any real clarity about the appropriate occasions for censorship, well, surely they could claim the consolation of very distinguished company in that failure.

Seven Justices, then, were ready for the Court to serve as the nation's aesthetician of last resort. Some called for a more aggressive role, some for a less; but none renounced that responsibility altogether. They were willing to act as censors. They put themselves forward as physicians to the American psyche. They held themselves out as ministers to the American soul.

What about the two Justices who wanted to abolish the office of censor? Were they, in fitting modesty, abstaining from soulcraft?

It isn't quite that simple, is it?

Granted, they wanted the Court to keep its hands off all literary and graphic productions — but they wanted more than just that. They wanted every public official in the nation to keep his hands off all literary and graphic productions. They were arguing, in effect, that the American soul would be better off, would be healthier and happier and more virtuous, under a uniform regime of artistic laissez faire. They were asserting that human beings have, if not an immunity to bad art, at least a sufficient resistance to make the effects of organized censorship inevitably, on balance, more corrupting than any work of art can be.

These two Justices, that is, also issued a prescription for the health of the soul, no less so than their colleagues.

All the Justices maintained that they were interpreting the Constitution of the United States. Once again, however, let us defer the constitutional question. Let us merely observe that two of the Justices were very plainly carrying new tablets down from the mountaintop.

CHAPTER 10: MEMORY ON TRIAL

In mid-twentieth century America, education at the elementary and secondary levels was most commonly provided by public school districts, of which there were thousands. These were small governmental agencies, each locally organized and administered pursuant to state statutes. Each offered schooling, practically cost-free, to all children and adolescents within a certain geographical area. Each had the power to tax within its boundaries. Each was supervised by a board of citizens who resided within the district, and who were elected by their fellow residents. Each had substantial authority over the content and character of its teaching; and collectively, they reflected the considerable variety to be encountered across a nation of continental extent. Numerous, heterogeneous, each relatively self-governing, together they provided, from the ground up so to speak, a basic education to most Americans.

Their independence was significantly diminished in 1948, however, when the Supreme Court of the United States decided that local decisions about curriculum can bear constitutional significance.

The district which was the focus of this unwanted judicial attention was providing, in cooperation with a citizen group representing the Protestant, Catholic, and Jewish faiths, very brief sessions of religious instruction. Half-hour weekly classes were held in the school buildings. Only pupils whose parents requested their child's participation attended. The instructors were selected and paid by the church or synagogue, but had to be approved by the public school superintendent. Pupils whose parents did not wish them to attend did not, and were provided alternative instruction or supervision.

Programs like this, designed to supplement a principally civic and practical education, were not unusual at the time.

Nonetheless, eight Justices declared the practice impermissible, as an excessive entanglement of church and state.*

Religion and education, in the West, had long been considered related and mutually supportive activities. Europe's universities were born within the cathedrals and monasteries of the Roman Church. One of a university's principal functions, well into the nineteenth century, was the training of a competent, and ideally a learned clerisy, to lead the churches and minister to the laity. In North America, from colonial times through the birth of the United States and beyond, this tradition continued. Religious and educational institutions often remained closely associated. Even when the distinction between church and state had assumed constitutional significance, accommodations were usually found between church and school.

The particular accommodation contested before the Supreme Court in 1948 was surely a modest one, by his-

---

* McCollum v. Board of Education, 333 U.S. 203 (1948)

torical standards. In putting an end to it — in vetoing any formal church presence in public school buildings — what were the Justices telling the American people?

They spilt much ink, of course, telling the American people that their Constitution required this of them. But let us postpone the consideration of that contention, which was quite novel at the time.

Let us ask, rather: What sort of pedagogy were the Justices prescribing for the great majority of American students, as of 1948?

The Justices' new pedagogy was one in which the subject of theism, of the meaning and the history of theism, is sharply curtailed, if not entirely eliminated; a pedagogy in which young Americans no longer learn much about this subject. Young Americans were henceforth to be raised up as good citizens of a representative democracy, understanding their nation and their governance, fulfilling their responsibilities as citizens, without necessarily encountering any committed, professing Christians or Jews.

This new educational program, however, has broader implications. America is part of the world, and Americans need to understand the world. The Justices, it seems, were confident that future citizens of the Republic could sufficiently comprehend the great pageant of world history, as of 1948, without any close or personal encounter with ideas which had inspired and driven much of that history. For eight Justices, apparently, the march of time had put theism in the way of extinction. Whereas so many human beings, perhaps most human beings, once were earnest about things divine, and yearned for the touch of divinity in their lives, the Justices implied that many fewer now do so; and soon, perhaps, fewer still. In the Justices' history, the world has changed fundamentally. The religious teachers and prophets of ages past once shaped cultures and swayed the fortunes of peoples. According to the Justices, however, the time for such things has passed. A little superficial exposure to the major world religions, perhaps their brief mention as quaint and curious phenomena, will be quite sufficient for most modern students. More would be a waste of time. That type of study, crowding out more important topics, might even be harmful. Good teaching practice, modern teaching practice, demands that the standard curriculum for most youths be improved by pruning away obsolete and extraneous information.

Surely the Justices were nothing if not bold, in assessing their historical moment.

But were they right?

History has never been known to take direction well from its individual participants. Historical projections are often seen, with the advantage of hindsight, to have been disguised personal or partisan predilections.

What if there is simply no way to know whether the Justices of 1948 were right or wrong, about the role of theism in a sound education?

A people's history, a people's understanding of its history, is analogous to a person's memory. Memory shapes character, both individual and collective. A substantial loss of memory can be depended upon to bring about a marked change in character, probably a change for the worse. If theism remains a living tradition, with power to move peoples and to shape destinies, then the nation which averts its eyes from that fact chooses ignorance over knowledge. If theism is a living tradition — if, in its various forms, it inspires individuals and organizes vibrant communities — then all young persons, not only Americans, have a compelling need to study its past, good and bad, and to become aware of its spiritual potency.

If the Justices were wrong, then they were prescribing for a great many young Americans a seriously defective education.

Right or wrong, however, the Justices' new pedagogy, having been made official and mandatory, began to nudge young Americans along different paths, supposedly better paths, to the good life; and to point them away from older paths, from paths now frowned upon by an avant-garde.

The Justices' 1948 ruling, whatever else it may have been, was not merely a constitutional interpretation, or misinterpretation. It was an exercise, on a national scale, of soulcraft.

This was an extraordinary day's work for the Supreme Court of the United States. In banning the teachings of many world-shaping leaders and prophets from the learning offered most American youths, the Justices made the teaching of a large domain of human affairs and history less common. Putting some of the central preoccupations and concerns of earlier generations off limits in the public schools, they made the struggles of their ancestors unnecessarily mysterious to many American citizens. The Justices hardly began, but they enthusiastically furthered, a gathering alienation from the nation's traditions.

And they did even more. Heavily ironic, but generally unnoticed, was the Justices' revival of a very old pedagogical practice and doctrine. In turning the central government of the United States into an educational authority — into something it had not been for its first one hundred and sixty years — they also, and unwittingly, turned the American nation back toward an ancient religious tradition. The Justices re-entangled church and state and school — at a governmental level where church and state and school had been deliberately disentangled in 1787. They did this, even as they simultaneously denounced the entanglement of religion and politics.

In putting memory, the nation's memory, on trial, did the Justices of 1948 presage their ruling on the topic of school prayer fourteen years later? Did they foreshadow their later addition of the American imagination to the American memory, as spiritual topics suitable for their jurisdiction?

CHAPTER 11: ORTHODOXY ON TRIAL

In 1937 the Supreme Court of the United States considered the plea of a man convicted of murder and scheduled for execution. He complained of the manner in which the State of Connecticut had tried his case. His counsel's arguments were not, ultimately, persuasive to the Court, but the circumstances were somewhat unusual: He had been tried twice for his crime.

Convicted the first time, he had been sentenced to life imprisonment. At the initial trial, however, some of the state's evidence against him had been excluded by the judge. The decision to keep that evidence from the jury moved the aggrieved prosecutors to appeal, and the result was a retrial in which the state was allowed to present its more complete case. At that second trial, moreover, the prosecution succeeded not only in convicting the accused, but also in convincing a new jury that capital punishment was called for.

What is a fair trial?

In reverse, perhaps, the question is more manageable:

What can make a trial unfair?

A judge or jury predisposed against one of the adversaries? Surely this must give us pause about a trial's outcome.

Procedural errors? Surely the suppression of relevant evidence, or of persuasive arguments, must also give us pause.

Consider criminal prosecutions, in which a government accuses someone of a grave offense against the community-at-large and seeks to deprive him of his freedom, or even of his life. In this special kind of trial, can special kinds of unfairness occur?

The American founders thought so. In 1791, they included in the Bill of Rights, the first ten Amendments to the Constitution, a prohibition of what came to be called double jeopardy: "nor shall any person be subject for the same offense to be twice put in jeopardy of life or limb ..."

Unsurprisingly, the convict described above, his appeals having failed in the state courts, looked beyond them and sought the benefit of this constitutional protection in the courts of the nation. A little surprisingly, perhaps, the Supreme Court ruled that he had not been twice placed in jeopardy — not, that is, in the sense forbidden by the Bill of Rights. Unperturbed by the state's presentation of a fuller case against him at the second trial, the Justices rejected his appeal. They weighed the erroneous handicapping of the prosecution in the first trial against the hardship and peril suffered by the accused in undergoing a second, and they judged that the balance had been reasonable enough.[*]

The Court judged, in effect, that here it had taken two attempts to get one fair trial; fair, that is, to both the

---

[*] Palko v. State of Connecticut, 302 U.S. 319 (1937)

accused and the prosecution.

The idea of fairness lay at the heart of this controversy. But the eighteenth-century authors of the Constitution and the Bill of Rights did not use that particular word; and this sent the Justices off on an interesting detour to their constitutional interpretation.

Pondering this alleged double jeopardy in 1937, the Justices sought some general principle, or some additional perspective, with which to frame their deliberations. The Justices found what they were looking for in the idea of liberty — in "the meaning, the essential implications, of liberty itself." Reviewing a number of their previous decisions, a collection of seemingly erratic applications of the Bill of Rights, they discerned the concept of liberty, or thought they discerned it, serving as an ordering or explanatory rationale.

The Justices' choice might have seemed natural enough. Liberty is one of the great ideals announced in the Preamble to the Constitution of the United States. It is one of the blessings sought for American citizens by the statesmen of 1787. The word appears in the Bill of Rights. The idea will be invoked easily and naturally, therefore, by judges charged with adjudicating cases and controversies arising under those venerable charters.

Should the concept of liberty, then, enjoy a presumptive precedence, in constitutional litigation, over the distinct concept of fairness? Whether it should or not, the Justices declared liberty their lodestar in this case.

They erred, however. If not immediately apparent, their error quickly became obvious. Arguing in support of their decision, they felt compelled to call upon a number of ideas and ideals, none of them mere synonyms for liberty. As the builders of the Tower of Babel were confounded by the shattering of their linguistic unity, so, we might say, were the Justices defeated in their attempt to make of this one word, liberty, a ladder with which they could scale the heights of justice.

Thus they found themselves, in the course of the opinion, speaking of order: "... the very essence of a scheme of ordered liberty." They were seeking the meaning of ordered liberty, it seems, not of liberty in its broadest sense.

They found themselves speaking of justice, of tradition, of conscience: "a principle of justice so rooted in the traditions and the conscience of our people as to be ranked as fundamental."

They found themselves speaking of reason — by reference, however, to its opposite: "the legislative judgment, if oppressive and arbitrary, may be overridden by the courts."

They found themselves calling upon the distinction between a law or rule, on the one hand; and on the other the procedures by which the law or rule is enforced. This is a notion given expression as the phrase "due process of law," in both the Fifth and Fourteenth Amendments to the Constitution.

They found themselves invoking the primal virtue of compassion or mercy, again in negation: "This is not cruelty at all, nor even vexation in any immoderate degree."

They found themselves resorting to the sublimely ambiguous ideal of equality: "A reciprocal privilege [of appeal] ... has now been granted to the state. ... The edifice of justice stands, its symmetry greater, to many, than before."

The Justices ranged far afield, in search of justifications for their ruling. This is not to say that they failed to persuade either themselves or their readers. Nor is it to say that they ruled unjustly.

Clearly, however, they failed to find in the idea of liberty, alone, the cogency they sought. They purported to place liberty itself on trial, and to ferret out of it those elements bearing upon the litigation before them. But this was misleading. In fact they were engaged in a brief canvass of numerous first principles embedded in their nation's history, its traditions, and its Constitution.

Yet there is a sense in which the Justices of 1937 did place liberty on trial in this case. Their ruling did not bind the State of Connecticut, or any state, to any one rule or standard regulating prosecutorial appeals in the course of criminal litigation. Connecticut might allow such appeals. Next-door, Massachusetts might not. Then, at a later time, Connecticut and Massachusetts might both change their laws, even reversing positions. The Supreme Court left Connecticut and Massachusetts at liberty, we might say, to interpret liberty differently in the matter of prosecutorial appeals.

According to the Justices' statement of their task, however, implicit in the very idea of liberty should have been a clear assessment of the fairness of reciprocal rights of appeal in criminal cases. That answer, once found, should then have pointed to their ruling, which would have become the law, uniformly, throughout the United States. But the ruling they handed down left the question just where they found it. They left that question to be decided state-by-state. Their ruling, given the existence at the time of forty-eight states in the American Union, guaranteed that there would be multiple answers, across the nation, to a single question about prosecutorial appeals in criminal trials.

Were there — are there — various plausible and respectable answers to this question of criminal procedure? Or is there one correct answer, fair and unique?

And, if fairness in this setting cannot be captured in a single rule, then, to that extent, should the various local governments have been left unhindered in their administration of justice?

This was the deeper question that the Justices were deliberating in 1937. They were grappling with a fundamental question about liberty — the issue of one way versus many ways — an issue which surely lies at the heart of any investigation into the nature of a liberal order.

Is there one liberty? Or are there different liberties, numerous liberties, even incompatible liberties?

To raise this question about liberty, moreover, implicitly raises it also about each of the additional ideals which the Justices invoked in 1937. Order, justice, tradition, conscience, reason, sound procedure, compassion, equality: Which is a mere corollary to liberty? Each seems to stand on its own, a sort of moral vertex toward which our conflicts and dilemmas often pull us. Each has a strong claim to be considered a first principle in itself. Each tends to elude any given verbal formulation.

And when we put one or more of these ideals or principles into play in addressing an issue of right versus wrong?

Then we are drawn ineluctably into a review of our experience. Then we are sent soaring into our highest reaches of imagination and reason. Then we are plunged into strong currents of intuition and sympathy. Amidst such perplexities, how can even the most reasonable and well-intentioned persons, caught up in the flux of circumstance and perspective, unfailingly agree?

One way versus many ways, one belief versus many beliefs, one ethic versus a variety of ethics: What the Justices were actually probing in 1937 was something even larger than the meaning of liberty. They were probing the idea of orthodoxy itself, and the proper place of orthodoxy in the American political dispensation.

But how, the reader may ask, could the Constitution have offered the Justices any real guidance in so large an inquiry?

Granted, the Constitution prescribed an orthodoxy directly relevant to the doomed convict's case: that no accused criminal in the United States, properly tried and duly acquitted, is to be retried for the same alleged offense. This salutary principle, however, does not explain itself. It retains some measure of ambiguity, an ambiguity sufficient to encompass the issue raised in 1937. This terse constitutional orthodoxy requires further elucidation.

Were the Justices, then, on their own? Were they left to search the American soul? To ponder human nature?

They were not; and one subtle but very telling omission betrayed their error. In referring at one point to the Bill of Rights, the Justices spoke only of Amendments 1 to 8.

No careful student of American history would say that — not without explaining his omission of Amendments 9 and 10.

The Justices, that is, in reviewing their constitutional texts, simply dismissed two provisions of the Bill of Rights, two amendments included in 1791 for the very purpose of guiding later interpreters. One of those forgotten provisions, moreover, the Tenth Amendment, was more than just relevant:

> The powers not delegated to the United States by the Constitution, nor prohibited by it to the States, are reserved to the States respectively, or to the people.

These few words, of course, could not answer the very specific question of criminal procedure before the

Court. They were much too general for that purpose. They bore weightily, however, upon the deeper question which was running, unacknowledged, through the Justices' deliberations in 1937.

Just how tight, how detailed, how comprehensive should the American orthodoxy on double jeopardy be? Should every alleged instance of double jeopardy in a criminal prosecution require resolution by the Supreme Court of the United States? Or should the understanding of double jeopardy be allowed some variability, according to the experience and the wisdom of different states?

The Tenth Amendment addressed the perennial problem — the religious problem — of orthodoxy versus heterodoxy. It made clear that the meaning of liberty, the American understanding of liberty in the late eighteenth century, had not been surrendered, not entirely, to the new central government. The Amendment made clear that Americans of the late eighteenth century, not only as to liberty but as to all the great ideals given expression in their political scriptures, accepted, and indeed expected considerable variation. The Amendment made clear that local American communities, political associations organized on a much smaller scale than the nation, had rights also.

The Tenth Amendment offered instruction to future generations against an error — the error of thinking that legal rights in the United States attach to individuals only, or concern individuals only. It established a legal presumption, or burden of proof. It declared that the rights of local governments were not to be abridged or denied except where the Constitution, or one of its Amendments, cogently requires subordination to the legitimate concerns and the properly enacted laws of the central government.

The Tenth Amendment, ignored by the Justices of

1937, was more than just pertinent to the specific issue before them. The Tenth Amendment set the philosophical background against which that narrower issue should have been deliberated.

More broadly: The Tenth Amendment, ignored generally by the Court in the twentieth century, is an integral and very important part of the Bill of Rights. The American founders were not given to empty gestures or wasted words — least of all, to wasted constitutional words.

Poor interpreters, then, of their text — of this, we may properly accuse the Justices of 1937. But if they read the letter carelessly, if they read it unhistorically, in their ruling they remained true to its spirit. They did not dictate to every state in the nation a debatable notion of fair procedure in criminal trials. They did not expect to extract from the Constitution an answer to every question, or a resolution of every conflict.

In light of later developments, moreover, we might be inclined to praise the Justices for remaining interpreters at all. They looked to their text, to their precedents, and to the history and the traditions of their nation. They submitted themselves to what they found. They did not presume to teach their fellow citizens new lessons about truth, about justice, or about human nature.

CHAPTER 12: THE FAMILY ON TRIAL, 1925

May a state government monopolize the education of children and adolescents? May it require every young person within its boundaries to attend schools administered by public officials and staffed by public employees?

Educational institutions in colonial North America, and in the early American republic, had been largely independent of government. In the nineteenth century, however, public school systems arose and quickly became widespread. Still, they never entirely replaced private and denominational organizations.

In 1922, however, the State of Oregon decided to make its common schools mandatory for all.

This must have shocked a good many parents who wanted their faith taught to their children. It must have shocked the clergy who expected to teach those children. Whatever the motivations behind it, certainly it presented the appearance of an attempt to marginalize the religious traditions cultivated in church-affiliated schools.

So bold an innovation could hardly have been expected, in the United States, to escape litigation. This one did not. Without delay, the Society of the Sisters of the Holy Names of Jesus and Mary, defying the state government's attempt to empty their school of students, sought protection in the courts of the nation.

And indeed, when the case reached the Supreme Court in 1925, the Justices ruled that Oregon's officials had overstepped their authority.*

In this struggle between a religious school and a state government, surely we would expect to find the Court discussing the First Amendment. Yet we do not. A little history helps us to understand why. The historical First Amendment, the literal First Amendment, gave the nation no authority over local religious policies or legislation; and the Justices, at the time of this controversy, still observed that limitation. As hostile as the Justices were to Oregon's aggressive educational initiative, the Bill of Rights, as then understood, offered them no help. This new state policy drove them, therefore, into abstractions and circumlocutions. They struck it down, upholding the right of parents and churches to operate private schools for children; but they spoke not at all about religion. They spoke about business corporations, about property rights, about personal liberty. They spoke about reasonableness versus unreasonableness, a very handy distinction when more specific reasons seem elusive, or ambiguous, or incompatible.

Except — one unguarded statement crept into the opinion. The State of Oregon's implicit contempt for parental beliefs, and its peremptory nullification of parental prerogatives, drew from the Court this rebuke: "The child is not the mere creature of the state." For a moment, a mere ten words, the judicial demeanor slipped. In the place of an august, black-robed jurist, legal text in hand, there appeared an alarmed parent. The Justices did not cite any statute, or any constitutional provision,

---

* Pierce v. Society of Sisters, 268 U.S. 510 (1925)

for this almost unmentioned point, this incongruous *cri de coeur*, the very crux of the case. But there it was.

Actually a citation was available, but not to a source much called upon in opinions of the Supreme Court of the United States:

> Honor thy father and thy mother: that thy days may be long upon the land which the Lord thy God giveth thee.

Had the Justices allowed themselves a discreet paraphrase of this part of the Decalogue — had they suggested that honoring parents requires some accommodation of parental choices and convictions — they might well have explained and highlighted their first concern and their truest rationale.

The rights of parents, the needs of children, the sanctity of the family — set these against the edict of a government, and strong passions will not be far to seek. Innovation here will guarantee conflict among any large population. Unanimity will be out of reach. Democratic consensus may even be difficult to achieve. These issues, if and when they become issues, will hardly be resolved by anyone's reading of a short text which does not address them, hallowed though that text may be. And the spare words of the Constitution of the United States do not address them, let alone attempt to resolve them.

The Constitution, that is to say, is silent here. It does not require, it does not even suggest, that the United States as a nation should favor public schools over private schools — or private schools over public schools, for that matter.

But, once again, the Constitution is not irrelevant. The Constitution pronounced no verdict upon Oregon's school consolidation of 1922. It did, however, point to Oregon, and to other states, as the settings in which such decisions should be made:

> The powers not delegated to the United States by the Constitution, nor prohibited by it to the States, are reserved to the States respectively, or to the people.

The Tenth Amendment — plus the omission of education from the authorities and responsibilities of Congress — plus the absence of any corresponding restrictions upon the state governments — these things speak clearly enough about the proper origin of educational orthodoxies in the United States. The power of legislation regarding families and schools was reserved in 1787 and 1791 to the local governments and their citizens.

Nonetheless, in 1925, in deciding whether a state government could put all the private schools within its boundaries out of business, the Justices brought forth a new constitutional prohibition: No state government may force all children to attend public schools.

Put a little differently: Educational orthodoxy in the United States of America allows and protects educational heterodoxy — as of that date, and until a later Supreme Court decides differently.

Did the Justices rule wisely here? Did they decide well?

Wisely or unwisely, well or poorly, we need to recognize both Oregon's attack on private schooling, and the Court's response, as religious actions. Teachers shape young characters, as do parents. Different settings and personalities are important. Choices must be made not only as to curriculum, but also among different emphases and styles. Any formal plan of instruction comprehends only a part of what is learned.

The education of children is an exercise in soulcraft; its organization and administration are exercises of religious authority.

Chapter 13: The Family on Trial, 1878

In the nineteenth century an American prophet, Joseph Smith, founder of the Mormon faith, promoted among his followers the practice of polygamy. This ancient (and not only ancient) form of marriage was illegal in the British colonies and the early Republic. Its open advocacy incited almost universal indignation. Its practice put most Americans and their political officials, local and national, quite out of temper. Hostility to it, and to the beleaguered Mormons more generally, drove them from place to place. Finally, far westward across the continent in sparsely populated Utah, they found by mid-century isolation enough to enjoy some peace and security.

So, for a time, Mormons did not much trouble their fellow citizens. As residents of a territory of the United States, they were allowed a measure of local self-government. The convulsions of the Civil War and its aftermath spared them the close attention of their countrymen. But polygamy was a crime, even in Utah; and in 1878 a Mormon bigamist, convicted under a Congressional statute and sentenced to imprisonment by a territorial court, took his plea for religious liberty to the nation's court of last resort.*

His plea, the Mormons' plea, fell on deaf ears. No argument that Mormons might offer in behalf of their law of marriage was going to appease the Court, or the Congress for that matter. Reasoned public debate about polygamy was not going to occur in that time and place. The outcome of the litigation was a foregone conclusion. The Justices saw nothing questionable at all in the Congressional prohibition. Their ire lending force to their words, they went straight to first principles.

No man's belief about the propriety of a law, said the Justices, can excuse him from the consequences of his deliberate violation.

Polygamy, said the Justices, has been regarded in all the northern and western nations of Europe not only as an odious practice, but also as one which predisposes a society to patriarchy and despotism.

The authors of the First Amendment, said the Justices, never intended the idea of religious liberty to encompass polygamy. This is shown by contemporaneous laws in all the colonies and states declaring it a crime.

Congress cannot pass any law restricting religious freedom, said the Justices, and Congress has not done so. Mormons may believe what they will, though they may not act accordingly.

Marriage law, said the Justices, is a foundation for civilization, and the prohibition of polygamy lies within the discretion of any government.

If not quite vehement here, the Court's tone was more than a little dogmatic. But the rhetorical aggression cannot conceal, indeed it suggests, some difficulties. We can hardly help noticing a few problems with the first principles put forth by the Justices in connection with

---

* Reynolds v. United States, 98 U.S. 145 (1878)

the topic of polygamy.

Does the fact that a practice has long been condemned and prohibited guarantee its perpetual disfavor?

Is polygamy, always, everywhere, under all circumstances, a morally reprehensible and socially destructive form of marriage? Among the Mormons, did it present so baleful an aspect?

Is the criminalization of polygamy, in itself, an element of religious establishment — an establishment of monogamy? Or is there something deeper than religion, even more authoritative, bearing upon the issue of monogamy versus polygamy?

Does the ideal of religious tolerance come into play here? Can a living religion be neatly confined within the realm of thought and imagination? Are human dignity and integrity compatible with browbeaten silence about one's firmest beliefs, and a fearful shrinking from the obligations implied?

The Congressional persecution of Mormon polygamists continued into the 1880s, and even intensified. So it came about that in two decisions in 1890, the Court approved additional measures of suppression, including confiscation of the property of the Mormon Church.* In one of those opinions appeared the following language:

> Bigamy and polygamy are crimes by the law of all civilized and Christian countries. They are crimes by the laws of the United States ... They tend to destroy the purity of the marriage relation, to disturb the peace of the family, to degrade woman, and to debase man. Few crimes are more pernicious to the best interests of society, and receive more general or more deserved punishment. To extend exemption from pun-

---

* Davis v. Beason, 133 U.S. 333 (1890); Mormon Church v. United States, 136 U.S. 1 (1890)

ishment for such crimes would be to shock the moral judgment of the community. To call their advocacy a tenet of religion is to offend the common sense of mankind.

Here the Justices, in so many words, accused Mormons of religious fraud. Faced with theists convinced that God condones and even blesses polygamy, they resorted to equivocation and invective. This was worse than unseemly; it was pretentious and arrogant.

Thus did both Congress and the Court make abundantly clear their determination to force an American religious sect into the surrender of an important doctrine.

It would be surprising if many of the Congressmen involved in these matters paid close attention to constitutional concerns. It would not be surprising if some of them winked at polygamists in private; but none of them was prepared to wink in public. Their political careers and ambitions, we may assume, often came first. Of most elected officials, most of the time, we would expect little more.

But we expect more from the nation's highest judicial officers. We expect them to consult the Constitution. Here they did not do so. Their remarks about the First Amendment were facile and shallow. They presumed to declare the intentions of the founders regarding a subject probably not on the founders' minds at all, even as they waved aside plain words about Congress and the free exercise of religion. Nor did they discuss any other provision of the constitutional text or the Bill of Rights. Perhaps, regarding the case as one above or beyond such concerns and considerations, they were tacitly invoking the ancient idea of natural law. Or perhaps polygamy so offended them that their legal training was forgotten and their logical faculties suspended.

This was unfortunate, for the Constitution had guidance to offer.

For one thing: Concerning territories of the United States, as distinguished from states, Article IV Section 3 empowers Congress to make "all needful rules and regulations." This is broad language. Within a state, Congress is authorized to act only as to specifically enumerated topics and functions — marriage law not among them — and is sharply confined by the religious prohibitions of the First Amendment. It is not clear that Congressional authority is similarly limited in the governance of a territory.

For another: Article IV Section 4 directs the United States to guarantee to "every State in this Union a Republican Form of Government." It was surely arguable, and the Justices had argued, that polygamy fosters patriarchy and despotism. If so, then polygamy would work against the character and the institutions of self-government, thereby bringing Article IV Section 4 into play.

Nor should another pertinent constitutional mandate be forgotten:

> The powers not delegated to the United States by the Constitution, nor prohibited by it to the States, are reserved to the States respectively, or to the people.

The Tenth Amendment concerns the rights of local political communities vis-à-vis the central government of the United States. The Mormon sect was such a community. The Mormon sect was politically organized under a territorial government, and it was actively asserting its rights in that capacity; specifically, a religious right to legalize polygamy.

How, then, should the policy of the Tenth Amendment bear upon that of the First Amendment, and vice-versa? How should both Amendments be harmonized with Article IV, Sections 3 and 4? Should the constitutional right of religious liberty, guaranteed to American citizens, only fully mature when a territory becomes a state?

These were the questions that lawyers and judges, confronted with the struggle over polygamy, needed to engage. A focus upon these issues would have enabled the Justices to act as jurists, rather than as legislators. Such a focus might well have suggested to them that they did not need to call down thunderbolts of wrath upon polygamists.

But the Justices took up sword and shield, joining Congress in a crusade against polygamy.

What, then, was the Justices' proper role, their constitutional role, in this case?

The easy answer, the abstract answer, is — to assess the constitutionality of the legislation. They were called upon to approve, or to strike down, what Congress had done to Mormon polygamists and to the Mormon Church. This is a correct answer, but it becomes more illuminating if we describe the Congressional action more adequately.

And what, exactly, had Congress done?

Congressmen had presumed to distinguish good marriages from bad marriages, wholesome marriages from unnatural marriages. Congress had declared, for the United States of America, an orthodoxy as to the proper form and the true meaning of marriage.

The Justices, then, were called upon to consider whether the Constitution permitted Congress, under any circumstances, to establish a national orthodoxy of marriage. This momentous question was not as well posed as it would have been if one of the states had legalized polygamy. But it was framed clearly enough.

The insistence upon such distinctions in this setting may seem a distraction. To many, the most obvious question of all cannot be avoided: Is polygamy a pernicious institution, or not? Does a sound assessment of human nature dictate its suppression?

An obvious question, granted; indeed the largest question of all. But it is a religious question. Congressmen, moreover, had already answered it most emphatically. The Justices were not required to follow in Congressmen's footsteps, nor should they have done so. They were only required to say whether Congress had acted within the scope of its constitutional authority in prohibiting polygamy. They were called upon to decide whether the Constitution, with its emphasis on religious liberty and local prerogative, preserved some space, in the United States proper or in its territories, for marital heterodoxy — indeed, for marital heresy.

And note carefully: If the Justices had struck down the Congressional actions, still, they need not thereby have either praised or condemned polygamy. Citizens of Utah could have remained free to change their minds and enact a law of monogamy. Citizens of other states could have remained free to permit polygamy, should the passage of time and the evolution of beliefs bring that about. The best forms and the highest purposes of marriage could have remained an open question, so far as the Court and the Constitution were concerned.

Orthodoxy or heterodoxy? What has the Constitution of the United States to say regarding so momentous an issue?

Is the Constitution itself, to some extent at least, an orthodoxy? If so, what are its articles of faith? How broad is their reach? How many of the controversies which agitate the human spirit can be reasonably brought within the compass of that political scripture?

The question especially: How much room is there in American life for religious heterodoxy?

These questions were posed with great force by the struggle over Mormon polygamy. Unfortunately, the Supreme Court of that day showed little comprehension of them; no more comprehension than the Supreme Court of 2015 showed in declaring a new marital orthodoxy on its own, independent of Congress and in direct contravention of numerous state legislatures.

So domineering are the religious passions that they can move us to redefine our words. They can cause us to forget what we have learned. They can blind us to what we see, and deafen us against what we hear. So powerful are these hopes and fears, so hidden their presuppositions, that reason gives way. We want to justify some way, somehow, so badly, our beliefs and our demands.

Late in the eighteenth century the founders of the United States tried to inoculate their new national government against the religious factionalisms and furies that had wrought such havoc in Europe. Less than a hundred years later, however, the bitter struggle over Mormon polygamy had already made clear that the American experiment in religious pluralism was just that — an experiment.

CHAPTER 14: AN AMERICAN HYPOTHESIS

One way? Or many ways? Uniformity or diversity?
Orthodoxy or heterodoxy?

A longing for freedom, a commitment to freedom, it
seems, should make our answer easy. How could a free
and numerous people all share a similar character and
interests, common customs, like perceptions, match-
ing strengths and weaknesses? How could a single approach to life arise and become pervasive, absent powerful incentives, indeed compulsions, toward conformity?

But then, must the same question not arise concerning the various ideals canvassed by the Justices of 1937?

Is there one proper way to bring order to a community? To hold the primal chaos at bay?

Is there one true justice? One clear right and one clear
wrong, in all circumstances?

Does one tradition stand above all others as the most
conducive to human flourishing?

Must two consciences, if they are focused and per-
ceptive, converge reliably to similar judgments?

Should two minds, well-schooled, reasoning carefully, always reach consistent conclusions?

Can the understanding of mercy be different in those who differ fundamentally?

And equality? Shorn of its mathematical formulations, does it dissolve into ambiguity? Are there different equalities, serving different purposes and different circumstances?

Few are likely to find these questions ill-framed, or unworthy of reflection. Few will answer confidently. Yet that may change, if we ask a related question: Is there one form, and one form only, that a good government can take?

Here the warm friends of some favored theory or comprehensive plan may well answer promptly. And they might put a few pointed questions of their own.

Isn't a government, they might ask, an ultimate authority, an authority of last resort?

Mustn't a government, in deciding a controversial issue, decide for all? How would any official or tribunal, presiding over implacable adversaries, obligated to decide, accomplish anything by ruling in favor of both?

Has a predilection for many ways rather than one way, for diversity over uniformity, ever been much in evidence in the seats of power or the halls of state? Isn't orthodoxy the natural, even the necessary character of governmental means and ends?

All good questions. Nonetheless, the statesmen who founded the American Republic managed to put a case for plural government before the world with exceptional force and clarity. They offered a detailed and pragmatic plan, one quite disappointing to any partisan of governmental uniformity, for the preservation of many ways, legal, political, and religious, among the American people.

One topic, moreover, illuminated especially well the novelties introduced in 1787. One topic, the first to be addressed in the Bill of Rights of 1791, shone the brightest of lights upon the letter and the spirit of the Constitution of the United States.

In their approach to that most sensitive of concerns, religion, the American founders created something new under the sun.

It is a common assumption that the First Amendment epitomizes American thinking about church and state. This is not a surprising opinion. Religion, the word, is used only once in the original text, the 1787 text, of the Constitution — in the prohibition of religious oaths as a condition of office in the new central government. Also suggestive is the prominence in the Bill of Rights of the famous sixteen words: "Congress shall make no law respecting an establishment of religion, or prohibiting the free exercise thereof."

By contrast, the implication, plain in historical context — that the preexisting and ample religious authority of the thirteen colonies was deliberately left with the new state governments — being tacit, is easily missed, or dismissed, by a modern reader.

These are slender beams to serve as pillars of constitutional architecture on so vital a concern. Slender beams indeed: although they stood firm, and bore most of the weight placed upon them, for a century and more. On a larger view, however, they did not stand alone. They could not have stood alone. The idea that the American founders offered no additional guidance about religion is erroneous. Their Constitution said a good deal more than that. But in order to hear, we have to have some idea what to listen for. We have to be alert to silences, as well as to speech.

What, then, was not said about religious politics, or political religion, in the constitutional texts of 1787 and

1791?

The controversies addressed in earlier chapters will serve to illustrate.

Thus: There was nothing in the new Constitution about love. There was nothing about marriage or family relations. There was nothing about the meaning of sexuality. There was nothing erecting a wall, moral or legal, around individuals, a wall beyond which local governments were to have neither concern nor authority.

There was nothing about the perennial tension between logic and compassion, between justice and mercy. There was nothing committing charity to the supervision of Congress.

There was no assignment of roles or rights to men and women, nor any attempt to set constitutional standards as to relations between the sexes.

There was modest attention, but no more, given to the crucial question of persecution — to the pursuit and punishment of persons thought threatening to the well-being of others. The origin and enforcement of penal codes was left mainly to the local governments.

There was nothing inviting Congress to act as the collective conscience of the United States. A legislator's conscience should always be engaged in his official conduct, of course. But the topics committed to Congressional authority were so sharply defined and so limited, that the enactment of moral judgments into law would necessarily occur mostly through state action.

There was nothing authorizing Congressmen to interest themselves in the sensitive topics of pregnancy, or birth, or infancy.

Regarding literature and the other fine arts, the administration of copyrights was the sole responsibility given to the central government.

There was nothing assigning the nation any role in educating the coming generations. The learning and character of the young, if governmental concerns at all, were to be locally addressed.

These omissions, these silences, speak volumes. These concerns predominate throughout so much of our lives. They are the focus of so much endeavor, the source of so many passions. In addressing them we shape ourselves and influence others. In them we find so many of our joys and our sorrows.

These concerns, among others, will animate any religious movement. They will lie at the heart of any religious stance or dispensation. As to none of them was Congress empowered to act. As to none of them were the state governments forbidden to act.

As to none of them, that is to say, was orthodoxy, a national orthodoxy to be created by Congress, either contemplated or written into the Constitution.

The various American state governments, then, as of 1787 and 1791, remained, to a considerable extent, what they already were. They retained their authority to enact religious legislation. The statesmen of Philadelphia made no pretense of having curtailed the religious authority of the various local republics from which the Union arose. So long as the new central government confined itself to those powers and authorities specified in the Constitution, there were going to be as many distinctive accommodations between church and state in the United States as there were states to be united. The ample field of action left to the local governments, and the differing peoples and cultures spread across the nation, would guarantee that.

Many ways, not one way only, diversity, not uniformity, heterodoxy rather than orthodoxy, were to predominate at that troubled intersection where politics and religion converge, said the American founders; and they were seconded by the American people of the late

1700s. There would be no one version of religious liberty prescribed for citizens of the United States. The First Amendment, in its sixteen words about religion, was a very brief summation of thoughts already expressed and policies already adopted. The few words of the First Amendment offered then, and offer now, little or no additional guidance from the American founders upon the subject of church and state, or religion and politics. Those few words offered reassurance to those who needed it, those who feared that the new central government of the United States would set in motion a sweeping consolidation of sovereign authority throughout the nation.

It is an exercise in futility to look for a theory of church and state in the First Amendment. The constitutional text which it amends, however, is a rich field for that inquiry.

Today, two centuries and more after the earliest citizens of the American Republic debated and drafted and voted upon these matters, we hear a great deal about secular government. We are taught to think such a government ideal, and to frown upon something we call religious government. The statesmen of 1787, although they did not speak in these terms, thought along these lines. They believed that the new government they were building for the United States, a central government, would not intrude itself into religious concerns. There is no evidence that delegates to the constitutional convention left Philadelphia thinking that they had set in motion an eventual attack upon the religious convictions or religious organizations of the American people, or a stealthy subversion of the religious authority of the states.

Permitting ourselves an anachronism, then, we may say that the text of the Constitution, as it left the hands of its drafters in 1787, represented the thinking of the American founders as to what form a secular government should take. A secular government, according to their Constitution, is only a portion of a government. Such a government will be secular or not secular, according to the list of authorities it exercises — those it has, and those it is denied. And we may look to the text of their Constitution — specifically, at the powers they withheld from the new Government of the United States — for the various types of governmental authority which they thought unrelated to the responsibilities of the nation-at-large, or too sensitive and contentious to be relinquished to the nation-at-large.

They built a secular government; but they did not mistake it for a general government, a government of unlimited jurisdiction. They left a major role, indeed more often a primary role, across a broad and vital range of concerns, to the local governments of the United States.

Today we forget. Today we have created a national orthodoxy, supposedly derived from the First Amendment. Today we say that all governments, municipal, state, and national, should strive for neutrality as to religious concerns.

Today we imagine that we have corrected an error on the founders' part — the error of leaving a large measure of discretion with the local governments regarding religion.

The Constitution of the United States presented a profoundly original response to the deep tension between church and state, a tension that troubled and at times convulsed Christendom from the time that Christianity became the official religion of the Roman Empire. The hypothesis framed by that Constitution — let us call it the American Hypothesis — might be put thus: A government in full, a government recognizing no limits to its concerns or its competence, will not be, and cannot be, a secular government.

Religious liberty through religious diversity: Was this a vision, glimpsed at least in outline by some of the statesmen who gave it institutional form? Or was it more a historical accident, resulting from the nation-builders' realization that the divisive topic of religious policy would have been one item too many on their agenda?

Deliberate or unplanned, it presented a remarkably sophisticated conception of the first of liberties, religious liberty. The religious freedom of a numerous and heterogeneous people was to be attained through a carefully structured plural republic, one in which numerous electorates offered myriad opportunities for sages and seers and prophets, of all sects and persuasions, to contend for the souls of citizens.

The relentless march of political and religious events would soon enough, of course, put this vision, or this improvisation, to the test. The idea that a system of distinct governments, their powers carefully described and separated, could work together as a nation even as they maintained an elaborate partition of their functions and responsibilities, would soon enough encounter the severe stresses which history has always in store.

How has the American Hypothesis fared in the two centuries and more since it was framed? Earlier chapters offer some pertinent evidence.

"But what is government itself, but the greatest of all reflections on human nature?"* This observation by one of the foremost statesmen of 1787, made in the course of promoting the Constitution he had just helped draft, raises several questions.

Did the highly compartmentalized new government of the United States depend, in turn, upon a correspond-

---

* James Madison, writing in No. 51 of The *Federalist*.

ing compartmentalization of human nature?

If so, is human nature amenable to such a treatment? Can men and women divide themselves, balancing one thought against another, one passion against another, one loyalty against another? Or is single-mindedness, a real yearning for the one true way, a real resentment of difference and dissent, always there, always watching, always waiting?

Did the soulcraft of the American founders, in reaching so deeply, come to rest ultimately upon religious foundations? Were the American political scriptures, in themselves, manifestations of a religious stance toward the world?

Is there something paradoxical in these scriptures? Can an orthodoxy in favor of heterodoxy endure?

Tensions between religion and politics were certainly not resolved by Americans in the late eighteenth century. Those tensions were, however, given a novel and ingenious treatment, and a wonderfully rich setting for the continuation of their ancient story. Political partisans and religious enthusiasts would surely continue putting one another on trial in the United States, sometimes with violent and even calamitous results.

CHAPTER 15: AN AMERICAN ALLEGORY

In each of the European settlements which arose in the 1600s along the Atlantic coast of North America, many immigrants, using techniques their ancestors had developed over centuries, prepared alcoholic beverages from the foodstuffs available to them. They used these liquors liberally in easing hardships, in sharing observances of life's occasions and passages, and in relieving the frequent tedium and isolation of pioneer life. Sometimes, of course, use became abuse, to the detriment of those involved and of the communities in which they lived.

Already, as the colonial era drew to a close, there were noted Americans trying to dissuade their countrymen from heavy indulgence in strong drink; but their voices were few and their influence small. The thirteen colonies which joined together against Great Britain in 1775 and won their independence in 1783 reserved to themselves most topics of law and policy, even as they made themselves a nation; and among their many retained authorities was public power over the production, distribution, and consumption of liquors. Nor in framing a new Constitution, in 1787, did Americans deliberate at all about these concerns. Questions about alcoholic beverages, problems caused by alcoholic beverages, to the extent that they interested the earliest citizens of the United States, were questions and problems for local governments.

By the 1790s there were churches in the United States which were discouraging the consumption of liquors by their members. The evils of drunkenness — "a sin which excludes from heaven" — became a topic for American preachers, and the best of them brought to bear all the eloquence which a nation filled with ministers could boast. Americans of a devout and spiritual cast of mind, of whom there were a great many, would give the anti-liquor movement a strongly religious character from its beginnings, but more worldly associations devoted to the suppression of strong drink also arose.

In the 1820s the first regional and national anti-liquor organizations appeared.* The Washingtonians, named for the father of the country, encouraged reformed and repentant drunkards to make public confession, and sent the most articulate and histrionic of their converts on far-ranging speaking tours. The Cold Water Army organized Sunday school pupils against alcoholic beverages, offering children the satisfactions of ribbons and rhymes and parades. The Independent Order of Rechabites of North America, and the Sons of Temperance, coupled the allures of a secret society — dues, ritual, regalia, a hierarchy of titles, help for members who encountered hardships — to abstinence from liquor. Out of the Sons of Temperance, moreover, came several off-

---

* Kobler, John: *Ardent Spirits: The Rise and Fall of Prohibition* (1973). A survey of the more colorful personalities, important organizations, and main events of the temperance movement (and of its opponents) from colonial times through the repeal of the Eighteenth Amendment in 1933. It is the source of the information presented in this chapter, except where other references are noted.

shoots, such as the Templars of Honor and Temperance, the Knights of Jericho, the Independent Order of Good Templars, the Order of Good Samaritans. In California the Dashaways, in Chicago the Temperance Flying Artillery, took up the fight; and elsewhere the Sons of Jonadab, the Unitarian temperance society, the Catholic Total Abstinence Union of Baltimore. The list could be expanded. Americans were energetic and inventive in associating for the improvement of themselves and others.

Early in the history of the Republic these widespread labors against liquor began to affect local elections. No vision of social improvement which appealed to numerous citizens of the United States lacked politicians to espouse it, nor laws framed to further it. In the 1850s, the temperance movement began to show real political strength. From 1850 through 1855, fourteen states or territories — Maine, Minnesota Territory, Rhode Island, Massachusetts, Vermont, Michigan, Connecticut, Indiana, Delaware, Iowa, Nebraska Territory, New York, New Hampshire, and Pennsylvania — attempted to suppress commerce in alcoholic beverages among their residents.* These first anti-liquor laws were novelties and experiments. Governments had long treated the trade, in all its branches, as sources of revenue. What government had ever undertaken to put an end to it? Two state supreme courts held prohibition statutes constitutionally defective, and in most of the remaining states they were soon weakened or repealed. Many Americans found too much pleasure in drinking, or too much profit in supplying drink, for such stern measures to be easily accepted.

For about a decade encompassing the Civil War years, controversies over liquor were relegated to the

---

* Kobler, ibid., pg. 88.

back of the public mind. The great national calamity, together with its prelude and its aftermath, necessarily diverted attention and energies from most other topics. Even so, the war was the occasion for one measure which would come to play a large role in temperance politics. The Union could not fight secessionists without a greatly augmented flow of funds; and Congress, among its revenue enactments, included in 1862 a tax on alcoholic beverages.* This tax was not repealed upon the conclusion of the war. On the contrary, its administration was improved and systematized, and it soon came to generate a substantial portion of the receipts of the central government.

But the Civil War was a diversion from the hostility which many Americans had come to feel towards liquor, not a resolution. Soon after Appomattox temperance leaders resumed their proselytizing of the two dominant political parties; and when they met a cold reception there, they started their own, the National Prohibition Party. Organized in 1869, the new party would offer Americans an alternative candidate for the nation's presidency for several decades.

The early 1870s brought a new initiative, a contagious enthusiasm called the women's crusade. Across the nation, bands of women kept vigil at saloons and other sites of liquor vending, where they prayed, sang, harangued customers, and sometimes so discouraged and disrupted trade that the targeted businesses closed their doors. For several years the crusaders enjoyed publicity and success, but inevitably they were defeated by the determination and adaptability of the merchants of strong drink. From their ranks, however, emerged another national organization, the Women's Christian

---

* Hamm Richard F.: *Shaping the Eighteenth Amendment: Temperance Reform, Legal Culture, and the Polity, 1880-1920* (1995). A study of the evolution of liquor laws in the United States. See Chapters 3 and 5 regarding the national excise.

Temperance Union, which would carry on the fight in more traditional and less flamboyant ways.

In the 1880s temperance leaders took up a new strategy. When they found legislators too susceptible to the blandishments of liquor manufacturers and dealers, they sought and frequently obtained popular referenda upon prohibitory measures. The results of such plebiscites sometimes pleased their sponsors, but more often not.[*]

By the 1890s both the National Prohibition Party and the Women's Christian Temperance Union were suffering internal strife and defections. There was much disagreement about strategy. Some foes of liquor, frustrated with third-party politics, proposed to try to work within the two established and dominant parties. Some proposed to focus their resources upon liquor only, while others continued to insist upon the importance of maintaining coalitions with a diversity of reform movements. Struggle and schism in the dry ranks during these years may have lulled vintners and brewers and distillers into complacency, but their opponents, temporarily in disarray, were far from defeated. In fact new temperance leaders, filling the vacuum created by the troubles of the older organizations, would prove much more successful than their predecessors.

The Ohio Anti-Saloon League, founded in 1893, grew into the Anti-Saloon League of America two years later and soon became a very effective pressure group. The League included attorneys in its leadership and kept lawyers on retainer. Its approach was hard-headed and pragmatic. The organization was run from the top down, a hierarchy rather than a democracy. Its leaders gave priority to effective enforcement of the many liquor regulations and prohibitions already on the books of numerous states and municipalities. They sought their battles, and fought them, saloon by saloon and dealer by dealer, and

[*] Kobler, op. cit., pg. 157.

grew by co-opting the many scattered citizen groups
trying to suppress the liquor trade. They systematically
gathered information from federal liquor tax collectors,
using it as evidence of violations. They employed private
detectives to gather additional evidence. They spon-
sored public prosecutions where possible, and private
legal action where public officials would not act. They
established publishing houses which produced a growing volume of pamphlets, periodicals, and books. They
pushed for local option elections, gradually enlarging
the dry areas within a number of states until statewide
prohibition became feasible. They generally ignored
personal consumption of alcohol, campaigning rather
against commerce in liquors and provoking less popular
resistance. They avoided political alliances, working to
elect any Democrat or Republican who would support
the cause. And they remained steadfastly a single-issue
group, refusing to dissipate their means or their energies in other areas. Through these tactics, applied per-
sistently and methodically, the Anti-Saloon League kept
the temperance cause constantly in the public eye and
steadily increased the movement's power. Although the
League opened an office in Washington, D.C. in 1899,
most of its people worked in its many state and local
chapters, and most of its resources were expended locally. The League prospered, turning popular concerns into
public policy by following the well-trodden paths that
American constitutional and political tradition offered
those who sought change — from bottom to top, from
city halls to state legislatures to the halls of Congress.

During the last quarter of the 1800s, and continuing
into the first decades of the 1900s, many thousands of
Americans across the nation were devoting time, energy,
and money toward the suppression of liquor commerce
and consumption. The movement had its saints, such as
Eliza Daniel Stewart of Springfield, Ohio, widely known

as Mother Stewart because of her work in behalf of northern soldiers during the Civil War. The movement had its saintly sinners, none more famous than Carrie Nation of Kansas, whose dramatic axe-wielding forays into saloons drew huge publicity and inspired several imitators. The movement had its multifaceted visionaries such as Frances Willard of the Women's Christian Temperance Union, a tireless advocate and organizer for female suffrage and much else. The movement had its lawyer-redeemers such as Wayne Wheeler, a peculiarly American type, a human engine powered by a blend of moral single-mindedness and legal cunning. The movement had its trophy friends such as Abraham Lincoln, a nondrinker who had supported persuasion but opposed legal coercion. The movement had its wealthy benefactors, such as John D. Rockefeller. The movement had its new towns, such as Harriman, Tennessee, and Prohibition Park on Staten Island in New York, where municipal charters and deed restrictions were framed to close all the usual portals through which strong drink entered a community. The movement even had a few martyrs. Essayists wrote, orators declaimed, congregations prayed, contributions were collected, marchers paraded, flags waved, bands played, year after year, as Americans poured their passions against liquor into the many political and legal channels available to them.

And all the while the friends and leaders of the liquor industry, many of them wealthy and well-connected, applied steady counter-pressures, often covert and sometimes corrupt counter-pressures, in support of their busy and ineradicable trade.

The effort would be very large, and out of all proportion to the gain, in trying to detail the year-by-year changes in the laws of the various American states as the fortunes of the temperance crusaders and the liquor industries waxed and waned over the decades following the Civil War. A general survey, however, of those laws as they stood in 1918 — the year when the issue of national prohibition, in the form of the Eighteenth Amendment to the nation's Constitution, was pending before the forty-eight state legislatures — is quite instructive.*

Liquor's American foes had grown very powerful by 1918, but nearly half the forty-eight states had rejected their harshest proposals. All of these states licensed vendors, all regulated the trade to some extent. Almost all of them accommodated the temperance movement so far as to authorize cities and counties to vote themselves dry. Almost all supported their dry communities with localized restrictions on the marketing and transportation of liquors. Almost all allowed citizens a role in the granting of liquor licenses, so that a particularly objectionable vendor or retail site could be prevented or closed down. But throughout these states most Americans who wanted an alcoholic beverage could still, without large efforts, legally obtain one, and they had shown themselves determined to preserve their right to do so.

At least one state, South Carolina, had tried vending alcoholic beverages through a governmental monopoly. The experiment was later abandoned, however.**

A slender majority of American states, on the other hand, had by 1918 forbidden commerce in strong drink within their borders. None of these states, moreover, afforded any option to their cities and counties to vote themselves wet. Still, there were important differences among them. Many expressly recognized in their statutes the citizen's right to use small amounts, non-commercial amounts of liquor, at least in the home. Many implicitly recognized the right of personal use by limit-

---

* Wheeler, Wayne: *Federal and State Laws Relating to Intoxicating Liquor* (1918). This author, a leader in the temperance movement, collected the pertinent statutes as they stood at the time of his book's publication.
** Hamm, op. cit., Chapter 4, pgs. 128-129.

ing the scope of their penalties to the manufacture or sale of liquors. Very few states ventured so far as to penalize the individual possession of an alcoholic beverage.

All the dry states made a few concessions. They permitted liquors used for medicinal purposes, for scientific or industrial purposes, and for sacramental purposes. These exemptions tempted some to evade the law, of course, and doubtless a druggist, a laboratory worker, a manufacturing owner or supervisor, a clergyman, could often be found to bend the rules.

A widespread readiness among Americans to bend the rules, and a not uncommon willingness to defy them, explain why the dry states devoted a great deal of attention to the problem of enforcement. Regulations and penalties of various kinds took up most of the space in their liquor legislation. All of the dry states prohibited the manufacture and sale of alcoholic beverages. Most of them also banned advertising and solicitation. Most of them condemned buildings used for vending, and vehicles used for transporting illegal liquors, as public nuisances subject to forfeiture or destruction. Most of them declared contracts for liquor purchases, and leases to clubs or saloons, unenforceable. Most instructed banks not to handle the notes and bills of participants in the forbidden commerce. Most required licensure and record-keeping by persons and firms handling legal alcohol, and surety bonding against regulatory violations. Most gave federal liquor tax records a privileged status as evidence in prosecutions. Many of these state governments sought to enlist private citizens in the struggle, in order to supplement the efforts and resources of their public officials. Some of them authorized prosecutions by privately employed attorneys and investigators. Some gave the family of a person injured through intoxication the right to sue those who supplied the liquor. Some punished a vendor more severely for supplying liquor over an objection from the customer's family.

All in all, the statute books of the forty-eight American states, by 1918, bulged with instructions and prohibitions and penalties on the topic of alcoholic beverages. Many thousands of Americans, during seven to eight decades of political struggle, had represented their fellow citizens as state legislators, and had played some part in fashioning and refashioning these laws. Beyond this body of law, moreover, lay another mass of legislation, compiled by another army of citizens — the ordinances of the cities and counties which many states allowed to set their own liquor policies. Americans had spoken to one another, and argued with one another, so long, in so many different settings, that the legal outcome, the rules and regulations, would have filled several volumes had they been compiled. The debates had been long and rambling, and often inconclusive. The results were certainly not tidy. But variety, contrast, many ways rather than one way, had been preserved. The variations and the contrasts seemed likely to sum up the achievements of a persistent and eventually potent political movement, drawing wide support from several generations of Americans, toward the suppression of alcoholic beverages. This was as much as the foes of liquor seemed likely to accomplish, so long as they had to work within the multi-jurisdictional framework which structured the politics of the United States.

Temperance issues remained very controversial, dividing the nation along several lines. All the dry states but two were west of the Mississippi or south of the Ohio, the two exceptions being in rural northern New England. Of the more industrialized states only two, Michigan and Indiana, had embraced prohibition. The crusaders against strong drink were mostly rural, agricultural, Protestant Americans, and they had pretty much carried the regions most receptive to their call.*

And yet, in 1919, the one hundred and thirty-seventh year of their Republic, citizens of the United States added to their Constitution its Eighteenth Amendment, which preempted the laws of each level of American government, national, state, and municipal, with a comprehensive ban on alcoholic beverages. In 1919 several volumes of American legislation, a century's accumulation of the conflicting judgments of myriad persons about liquors, a complex, conflicted monument to the ideal of local self-government, was superseded by just fifty-four most uncompromising words:

> After one year from the ratification of this article the manufacture, sale, or transportation of intoxicating liquors within, the importation thereof into, or the exportation thereof from the United States and all territory subject to the jurisdiction thereof for beverage purposes is hereby prohibited.

If to simplify is to progress, then Americans progressed so swiftly regarding this vexing matter one fine day in 1919, as to find themselves once again living in a New World.

Then, only fourteen years later, Americans nullified their eighteenth constitutional amendment with their twenty-first, restoring public authority over strong drink to their various states.

What had happened? Was there ever a real consensus among the American people in favor of prohibition? If so, what persuaded a majority of them that they must insist upon uniformity in liquor policy? What then persuaded a majority of them so quickly that they must not insist upon uniformity in liquor policy? How did they

---

* Kobler, op. cit., pg. 217

come to treat their nation's Constitution as if it were a municipal code, to be cast into some strict and punitive form amidst the clamors of an unusually aggressive faction; and then, with a shift in the political currents and the intervention of an election or two, simply purged of the offending provision?

The historical record is voluminous; and though it may leave many questions unanswered, it readily discloses several unifying forces at work in the politics of liquor. Both those who condemned strong drink and those who defended it sought, in various ways, to overcome the obstacles to their purposes thrown up by numerous local authorities.

Among the advocates of prohibition were many true believers, fervent and impatient souls whose anguish over lives blasted and families impoverished was real enough. To many Americans, their nation's history and circumstances seemed to place it in the vanguard of human progress. The millennium seemed to beckon — a promised land where all would live in freedom and health and happiness and harmony. Many thought they saw a way, a path which could be traveled, from the ever-disappointing cities of man to the City of God. Some Americans saw in intoxication not just a weakness, not just a vice, but a sin; and saw, in supplying the means for that sin, not just a sin but the work of the devil. The idea of a world without liquor, at least of a nation without liquor, the deprecation of partial and local measures — a fixation upon the right way, the true way, the only way — came naturally and appealed strongly to many of these men and women. Nor was it mere coincidence that the first general measures to suppress liquor were enacted when a kindred wave of social reformers, the antislavery activists and abolitionists, were winning their local battles and raising their eyes to more distant horizons. Thoughtful Americans shared painful memories of the great cataclysm which had arisen out of the practice of involuntary servitude. Thoughtful Americans reflected, indeed many brooded, upon the lessons of that struggle. History offered an analogy — the drunkard as slave, alcohol as his chains, the distiller and tavern keeper as his masters — which foes of liquor could and did proclaim.

The ideal of the one way, the right way, beckoned temperance leaders when they organized the National Prohibition Party. The Party's existence, and its quadrennial quest for the presidency of the nation, suggested to Americans that their states were not adequate governmental authorities for the job to be done. In 1884 the Party would reach the peak of its influence, drawing 150,000 votes out of some 10,000,000 cast and very likely depriving the Republican candidate of victory.[*]

The idea of one true way was inherent in every proposal for a prohibition amendment to the Constitution of the United States. The first of these, but not the last, was introduced in Congress in 1876.

The one and only way forward was a recurring theme of the Women's Christian Temperance Union, founded in Cleveland, Ohio in 1874. Although members of the WCTU worked hard at the state and local levels and achieved much there, especially in the area of temperance education, their leaders were early advocates and agitators for national prohibition.

Thus was the demand for uniformity heard early and heard often on one side of the controversy. What about those who enjoyed alcoholic beverages, or profited from them, or at least approved of their use? What might have explained their opposition to local choice and legal diversity?

No single motive or idea, of course, drove those who defended the right to drink and the right to trade in

---

[*] Kobler, ibid., pg. 156

drink. Many of them were adherents to an orthodoxy which was quite powerful in their day, the faith in open markets, and the corollary to that faith, hostility to regulation and taxation. Commercial life had changed substantially since the days of the early Republic, and in ways which posed challenges to local governments. Americans were thinking on a larger scale and attempting more wide-ranging projects. Large-scale manufacturing, and swift distribution across vast distances, became possible in the United States in the second half of the 1800s. The entrepreneurs who arose to pursue these opportunities were little inclined to respect or abide provincial interference. Many distillers and brewers never desisted from shipping their wares into dry states. Many sent agents and salesmen into forbidden territory seeking customers. Many scorned demands that they impose some standards upon the premises and the persons through which their goods were sold. The makers and merchants of strong drink had little need to defy the law, however, because evasion was generally easy; and each illicit beverage sold in a dry area was another provocation to their opponents, whose natural response was frequently to call for a stronger law, a more comprehensive law — a national law.

Powerful proponents of a nationwide market in alcoholic beverages were found also in the Internal Revenue Office of the Treasury Department, the agency charged with administering and collecting the national excise. Federal revenue officials — their jobs making them accessories to the liquor commerce, their daily labors involving association and sometimes friendship with manufacturers and dealers — had strong incentives to dislike state and local prohibition, and many acted accordingly. Often they obstructed access to the information in their files, information quite useful to those seeking to prosecute violators. Often they refused to appear in state courts to testify about the activities of those from whom they collected the tax. Sometimes, when they seized inventories from dealers who tried to avoid the tax, they auctioned the condemned goods at the nearest federal facility — an act which, in dry jurisdictions, had the effect of granting a temporary exemption from local law to any citizen who wished to stock up on beer or wine or distilled spirits. Each defiance of state or municipal law by a federal official was a boast of superiority and an insult flung in the face of the temperance movement.*

Indeed the liquor tax itself, in addition to the bureaucracy which administered it, was to some extent an impetus to uniformity. The idea that two distinct governments, sharing concurrent jurisdiction over the same citizens and the same territory, might adopt contradictory policies toward the same commodity — one government taxing sales to raise public revenue, even while the other government tried to prevent any sales — was confusing to many Americans. The ambiguities generated by this legal bifurcation kept lawyers well employed, and drove others to demand simplification.

Yet neither the intemperate passions of the purists against liquor, nor the thirst for markets and profits of the makers and sellers of liquor, nor the arrogance of the revenue officials whose interests were coupled so closely to those of the liquor industry, nor the occasionally frustrating oddities of the federal system, nor even all of these together, would likely have overcome the decentralization of American liquor law. The states and cities of the United States were vibrant and resilient political institutions. The notion of the one true way, the drive to simplify and consolidate, had too many American opponents to vanquish and too much American history to overcome, to make much headway without very special

---

* Hamm, op. cit., Chapters 3 & 5

friends in key positions.

Among all the many causes and groups and interests which importuned American governments, those who defended the legality of alcoholic beverages had the good (or bad?) fortune to find such special friends. The biggest obstacle to local regulation of liquors, and the most provocative to the temperance movement, draw- ing Americans to Washington, D.C. again and again from 1890 onward, was the Supreme Court of the Unit- ed States. This singular institution, the smallest of the three branches of the national government and the most insulated from popular concerns and passions, was of- ten little affected by political pressures. The Court could reinterpret the nation's history, and sometimes refash- ion its laws, with considerable freedom and impunity. Over the quarter century which preceded national pro- hibition, the Justices of the Court took the lead in pre- venting the effective enforcement of state and municipal laws. They seemed strangely antagonistic to the temper- ance movement, and unaccountably attentive to the li- quor industries. Leaving the two factions to battle it out in multiple smaller theaters of contention rather than nationwide, as earlier Justices had done for decades, was for some reason no longer on the Court's agenda.

Controversies over liquor regulations first reached the Court in the 1840s; and in 1847, in a set of cases called The License Cases, the Justices unanimously affirmed the plenary power of each state to set its own policy re- garding the problems caused by alcoholic beverages.* To the antebellum Court, a state's suppression of the trade raised no questions under the Constitution.

Immediately following the Civil War, the nation's taxation of a commodity illegal under some state laws brought one such law before the Court. In 1866 a citizen

---

* The License Cases, 46 U.S. 504 (1847).

of Massachusetts, Mr. Pervear, sought there the nullification of his conviction in state court for prohibited sales of liquor.* His attorneys argued a proposition of logic: that the national tax, and his payment of that tax, made his business legitimate and thereby preempted the Massachusetts statute. The Justices responded unanimously however, that the national government's taxation of Mr. Pervear's sales conferred no immunity upon him against prosecution for violations of local law.

In 1873 an Iowa citizen named Bartemeyer asked the Court to overturn his conviction for selling whiskey. Mr. Bartemeyer found no friend among the Justices.** The Justice who wrote the Court's opinion drew no dissent when he said "We think that the right to sell intoxicating liquors, so far as such a right exists, is not one of the rights growing out of citizenship of the United States."

In 1877, the Boston Beer Company challenged the Commonwealth of Massachusetts, which had legislated an end to the brewing business. The company argued that the new state law illegally revoked its charter, a franchise granted by the state government five decades earlier, for "manufacturing malt liquors in all their varieties in the city of Boston." The Court did not agree.*** The state, said the Justices, may change its mind, and its law, as to what best serves the health and welfare of its citizens. Again, no Justice dissented. But a note of ambivalence, an omen perhaps for those who augured such matters, crept into the opinion: "Of course, we do not mean to lay down any rule at variance with what this court has decided with regard to the paramount authority of the Constitution and laws of the United States, relating to the regulation of commerce with foreign na-

---

* Pervear v. The Commonwealth, 72 U.S. 475 (1866)
** Bartemeyer v. Iowa, 85 U.S. 129 (1873)
*** Boston Beer Company v. Massachusetts, 97 U.S. 25 (1877)

tions and among the several states, or otherwise."

In 1887 the state of Kansas and one of its citizens came before the Court. Mr. Mugler had been a brewer prior to his state's prohibition law. He continued brewing and selling beer subsequent to that law, and was convicted and fined for doing so. Eight Justices upheld a state's authority to close a brewery and criminalize the selling of beer.* One Justice, however, expressed doubts. The dissenting Justice suggested that a state might exceed its authority in prohibiting the manufacture of liquors intended for sale in other states, or in prohibiting the sale within its borders of liquors imported from other states. He argued, moreover, that a state did exceed its authority in treating liquors, and the facilities in which liquors were made, as public nuisances subject to seizure and destruction.

One Justice out of nine cannot change the law. Thus far the American liquor industry, in all its various forms, remained a commercial activity which one state could allow and regulate, even as another state suppressed all production and trade. But the dissent in Mugler's case was a sign of change, and the change it signified was not long in coming.

Iowa was unusually aggressive against intoxicating drink; and among that state's restrictive measures was an 1886 statute requiring transport companies carrying liquors to verify the right of the recipient to sell them. Mr. Bowman, a dealer in Marshalltown, Iowa, went to Illinois, bought five thousand barrels of beer, and took the beer to the Chicago & Northwestern Railway Company for shipment to his warehouse. The railway company asked him for the certificate of authority required by Iowa law, and when he could not produce one, declined to accept his goods. Bowman then disposed of the beer for the price he had paid and sued the railroad

---

* Mugler v. Kansas, 123 U.S. 623 (1887)

for his lost profits. He got his case before the Supreme Court in 1888; and the outcome, surprising in view of the relevant legal precedents, was that Bowman won.* Six Justices struck down the Iowa statute and with it the railroad's defense to Bowman's suit. Shipments of liquor may move freely across state boundaries, whatever the legal status of the liquor upon delivery, said the Court. Congress, said the Court, could authorize such a law as Iowa's, but Congressional silence on the question must be interpreted as disapproval.

The ruling in Bowman's case was a puzzle. Four Justices, one in concurrence and three in dissent, were indeed puzzled. They pondered what the right to import liquors from another state could mean, if detached from the right to sell those liquors once imported. The three dissenters wondered how the silence of Congress regarding liquors could be interpreted as an intent on the part of Congressmen to curtail the authority over liquors traditionally wielded by individual states. The majority Justices did not explain; they were content to defer the questions they had raised to another day. The constitutional allocation of authority between central government and local governments over a widely controversial commodity, an allocation reasonably clear for a hundred years, had now been muddled.

Into the confusion in U.S. liquor law created in 1888 by the Supreme Court rushed new cases, as air rushes into a vacuum; and in 1890 the Court found an occasion to state plainly the diminishment of state authority which had been suggested, but not explained, two years earlier. Mr. Leisy, like Mr. Bowman, was an Iowa dealer who handled beer brewed in Illinois. Leisy, unlike Bowman, succeeded in getting his shipment of beer to its Iowa destination — where it was seized by Mr.

---

* Bowman v. Chicago & Northwestern Railway Company, 125 U.S. 465 (1888)

Hardin, an Iowa constable. Leisy, again like Bowman, soon got his suit up for review before the nation's highest tribunal and won his case.* Absent explicit Congressional legislation to the contrary, said six Justices, the interstate commerce clause of the United States Constitution confers upon Mr. Leisy a right not just to import his beer from another state but the right to sell it in his own state, Iowa, despite the Iowa statute forbidding that sale. For a hundred years the right to sell liquors had not been an incident or privilege of United States citizenship. Now, suddenly, it was; and there was no shortage of citizens ready, willing, and able to make full use of the new right.

The decision in Leisy's case, unlike the ruling in Bowman's, was quite clear. It was also a seriously unsettling change, given the antagonisms then roiling many citizens and regions of the nation. Three Justices of the Court dissented, protesting vigorously and at length the Court's repudiation of forty years of its own doctrine. The dissenters found no indication that the intentions of Congress as to liquor regulation had changed from 1847 to 1890. They could see no good reason for the Court to decree a sudden reallocation of authority over alcoholic beverages.

And what an odd right the Court was fashioning, this new constitutional entitlement which citizens of the United States would henceforth enjoy. Half the citizens of Iowa, plus one more, the barest of majorities, would be allowed to stop Mr. Bowman or Mr. Leisy from brewing beer in Iowa to sell there. Ninety-nine percent of the citizens of Iowa, however, would not be allowed to prevent the sale there of beer brewed in neighboring Illinois. Iowans, whatever the strength of their opinions, however widely they shared those opinions, would have to allow commerce in liquors to go on among them un-

---

* Leisy v. Hardin, 135 U.S. 100 (1890)

less they could persuade every resident of their state not to drink. Iowans had seen the Supreme Court demote their elected representatives, on the subject of alcoholic beverages, from legislators to subordinate officials of the central government. So had the citizens of every other state in the Union.

Congressmen were watching these developments and hearing from constituents. Few of them, it seems, Congressmen or constituents, were pleased. The Supreme Court had named Congress as the author, in spirit if not in letter, of the Court's innovations in liquor law. Congress had yet to speak about the subject, but now did so with surprising swiftness. Little more than three months after Mr. Leisy succeeded on defying the people and the legislators of Iowa, the legislators of the United States declared their intentions:

> Be it enacted by the Senate and House of Representatives of the United States of America in Congress assembled, That all fermented, distilled, or other intoxicating liquors or liquids transported into any State or Territory or remaining therein for use, consumption, sale or storage therein, shall upon arrival in such State or Territory be subject to the operation and effect of the laws of such State or Territory enacted in the exercise of its public powers, to the same extent and in the same manner as though such liquids or liquors had been produced in such State or Territory, and shall not be exempted therefrom by reason of being introduced therein in original packages or otherwise.[*]

A majority of Senators and Representatives, few of them strangers to the pleasures of a drink, many of them

---

[*] U.S. Statutes at Large, Vol. 26, pg. 313 (Wilson Act, 1890).

no enemies to the liquor industry, apparently saw little good likely to come from putting liquor controversies on the agenda of the nation. Congress was comfortable with the status quo, a status quo which had served Americans at least adequately, perhaps better than adequately, for a century.

Still, Congressmen stopped short of forbidding the transportation of liquors into states where the sale of those liquors was illegal.

American liquor law was now in disarray. Two of the three branches of the national government had issued pronouncements which, if not contradictory, certainly ran in opposing directions. Manufacturers, railroads, merchants, and state legislatures had ample reason for confusion.

Very shortly the Supreme Court returned to the question. In 1891 the Court decided a case governed by the Congressional legislation. Six Justices approved, with reservations, the prosecution of a liquor merchant named Rahrer by the State of Kansas.* Mr. Rahrer was the Kansas agent of a Missouri dealer, so the goods he sold were imported, bringing him under the rule in Leisy's case. But Congress, said the Justices, clearly intended to allow a dry state to prevent the sale of imported beverages. Therefore Rahrer's prosecution must be allowed. However, said the majority, the legality of the act of importation remains an open question. The Court retreated only so far as the enigmatical distinction first made in Bowman's case in 1888. The Justices were not ready to relinquish their solicitude for interstate commerce in liquors, nor were they much troubled by the continuance of a destabilizing legal ambiguity. They left the nation's liquor law unclear, and invited the liquor industry and the temperance movement to keep trying.

Neither of the contending factions needed an in-

---

* Wilkerson v. Rahrer, 140 U.S. 545 (1891)

vitation, but six years passed before some clarity was restored. Mr. Donald, a citizen of South Carolina, provided the occasion when he ordered a case of California wine, a case of Maryland whiskey, and a barrel of New York beer; all of which was confiscated by Mr. Scott, a South Carolina constable. Donald sued Scott for damages and won a judgment in the lower courts; and when he reached the Supreme Court, in 1897, his judgment was allowed to stand.* Seven Justices now found a way to bend the Court's doctrine of interstate liquor commerce before the political winds that were blowing, but still to keep that doctrine standing. Had Congress nullified the judicially-created right to sell imported liquors in defiance of local law? Congress had said nothing about importing and drinking out-of-state liquors. The Court now articulated the distinction. And in 1898 any ambiguity was resolved, when the Court reversed Iowa's conviction of a railroad station agent named Rhodes for delivering a package of liquor to an Iowa resident.** Six Justices now declared a state's prohibition of commerce in liquors ineffective against alcoholic beverages entering the state for personal consumption.

The Donald and Rhodes cases furnish a classic illustration of judicial inventiveness in support of judicial assertiveness. If Congress had subjected sales of liquor to state laws, a restriction which the Justices plainly opposed, why not shift the emphasis to purchases of liquor? Much could thus be salvaged. In a nation increasingly knit together by easy communications and transportation, an individual right to buy and receive and drink liquors must carry with it — absent one uniform national law to the contrary — a right on the part of liquor vendors to sell and ship those liquors. Such a right opens cities and counties and states to a nationwide

---

* Scott v. Donald, 165 U.S. 58 (1897); Scott v. Donald, 165 U.S. 107 (1897)
** Rhodes v. Iowa, 170 U.S. 412 (1898)

market. That market might have to be less efficient than it could be; but so long as a few states remained havens for the production of strong drink or for the importation of foreign beverages, entrepreneurs basing their operations there could supply the liquid goods which many Americans, in all regions of the nation, sought to buy. A flourishing trade could thus be maintained, even in the face of powerful political opposition.

There now followed a long decade of skirmishing in American liquor law, as the industry adapted its trade to exploit the new legal environment, and as temperance leaders sought new state laws and tried to get additional legislation through Congress. Meanwhile the Justices handed down a series of cases protecting the Court-created privilege of interstate liquor retailing. A state's attempt to complicate liquor purchases to the point of impracticability by requiring analysis and approval of imported beverages by a state chemist; a state's prosecution of the carrier of a cash-on-delivery shipment as an agent of the seller in collecting the price, and hence an illegal seller; a state's classification of railroad station houses as liquor vending sites, and therefore nuisances under state law; a state's conviction of a carrier for knowingly delivering out-of-state liquors to a habitual drunkard — all these fell at the hands of a majority of Justices from 1898 to 1909.[*] And in 1912, a unanimous Court held once again that a railroad company which declined to accept liquor consignments for delivery to residents of dry states or areas must answer in court for its refusal.[**]

Congress was not idle during this time. Many Rep-

---

[*] Vance v. Vandercook, 170 U.S. 438 (1898); American Express Co. v. Iowa, 196 U.S. 133 (1905); Adams Express Co. v. Iowa, 196 U.S. 147 (1905); Adams Express Co. v. Kentucky, 214 U.S. 218 (1909).
[**] Louisville & Nashville Railroad Co. v. Cook Brewing Co., 223 U.S. 70 (1912)

resentatives and Senators, few if any of them hostile to commerce, nonetheless had to face elections in which hostility to this particular commerce played an important part. The number of their concerned constituents had been growing, and the passions on both sides of the issue were intensifying. One statute, aimed at the interstate traffic which had arisen under the protection of the Supreme Court, made it into the books in 1909.* The new law required plain labeling as to contents and recipient, and prohibited collection of the purchase price by the carrier. This was a little ambiguous. Congress could have been understood as ratifying the work of the Court, and as merely refining the provocative practices of some sellers of the controversial goods. But Congress was not finished with its efforts.

In 1913, the ongoing struggle over liquors led to another Congressional enactment, the second to present an impression of strength and resolve:

> Be it enacted by the Senate and House of Representatives of the United States of America in Congress assembled, That the shipment or transportation ... of any spirituous, vinous, malted, fermented, or other intoxicating liquor of any kind, from one State ... into any other State ... which said ... intoxicating liquor is intended, by any person interested therein, to be received, possessed, sold, or in any manner used, either in the original package or otherwise, in violation of any law of such State ... is hereby prohibited.**

The force of this declaration was shortly amplified even more, for when the President vetoed the bill, Congress quickly summoned the necessary two-thirds ma-

---

* U.S. Statutes at Large, Vol. 35 Pg. 1136 (regulating interstate liquor shipments, 1909)
** U.S. Statutes at Large, Vol. 37 Pg. 699 (Webb-Kenyon Act, 1913)

jorities in both chambers and overrode his veto.

Yet the meaning of this latest statute was still not entirely clear. Congress, not the Supreme Court, was empowered by the Constitution to set the terms of interstate commerce. Congress was certainly not blessing the liquor industry's defiance of state and local governments. Plainly many Congressmen continued to be uncomfortable with the nationwide market in alcoholic beverages which the Justices had created. Twenty-five years of Supreme Court rulings on the vexed and divisive subject, however, had not persuaded Congressmen to make the mere commercial carrying of liquors into dry states illegal.

And the Justices persisted.

A resident of Kansas named Kirmeyer, a liquor dealer who split his operations — office and warehouse on the Missouri side of the Missouri River, stables and horse teams on the Kansas side — in order to circumvent Kansas prohibition, was convicted in state court of illegal retailing, and got his case before the Supreme Court in 1915. He went away an exonerated man.* Mr. Kirmeyer admitted that the sole purpose of his peculiar business arrangements was to evade Kansas law. No matter, said the Justices — because he was engaged in interstate commerce. No matter also, said the Justices, that his conviction would be allowed under the statue enacted in 1913 by Congress — because Kirmeyer's prosecution had begun in 1910. The Court stood by its earlier rulings. Offered another chance to correct their misreading of Congressional intent as to interstate commerce in liquors, and to moderate if not abandon their ventures in liquor policy, the Justices did not choose to do so.

In another 1915 case, this one litigated under the 1913 legislation, the Justices struck down Kentucky's conviction of the Adams Express Company for delivering li-

---

* Kirmeyer v. Kansas, 236 U.S. 568 (1915)

quors to residents of a dry area.* They sharply restricted the scope of that latest Congressional enactment, limiting its application to states which penalized the consumption of alcoholic beverages by individuals in private settings. Few states went this far. Under this interpretation the interstate retailing of liquor could continue throughout most of the nation, under the protection of the federal judiciary. The Court would allow a state to go dry, but only, in the vernacular of the time, by going "bone dry." The Court required a dry state to radicalize its liquor policy to the very limits of the possible, or to accept an extensive evasion of its liquor laws.

Thus was the liquor industry's national market kept pretty much intact.

By 1915, Americans had been arguing among themselves about liquor for more than a century. They had posed themselves, again and again, novel questions, questions raised by the conjunction of American social circumstances and American political forms. Which of the various state dry laws, in all their variety, would have proven workable? Which would have retained popular support if effectively enforced? Were there that many Americans who really hated liquor enough to force their fellow citizens to prepare their own potions or travel to another state? Could the arts of fermentation and brewing and distilling, refined and transmitted by generation after generation, really be suppressed among a large and technically advanced population? Could commerce in the fruits of those arts, considered desirable by so many, really be purged from wide expanses of a continent?

From the inception of the struggle until 1890, answers to these questions, tentative answers, had been proposed locally, had been very diverse, and had been

---

* Adams Express Co. v. Commonwealth of Kentucky, 238 U.S. 190 (1915)

in flux in many of the settings in which they were being tested. In fact the early prohibition laws had generated in many states an opposition equal to the task of weakening or repealing them. Beginning in 1890, however, and continuing until 1915, important questions about liquor laws were ruled out of order by the Supreme Court. The Justices had not presumed to answer fully, but they had limited the terms of debate and narrowed the range of permissible action.

The Court would no longer, after 1915, try to fashion a national law on this topic. Events would now move swiftly, placing other leaders and other institutions in the forefront. But the Justices, a bare handful of citizens in a republic of a hundred million persons, had led the way in nationalizing the controversy. For a quarter century they had shielded the liquor industry from political forces which would have closed off many of its markets. The industry remained relatively unhampered by the lines of demarcation which separated the multiple authorities of American government. The Justices had frustrated repeated attempts by state legislators, by state executives, by city and county officials, by private groups, and by Congress, to empower local communities to close themselves to that commerce. Their rulings radicalized those involved in the struggle. Each time the Justices struck down a state liquor law, they furnished anti-liquor firebrands a conspicuous platform from which to demonize a distant authority, and spared anti-liquor agitators the shock of confronting the problems of strict prohibition in their own states. Each time the Justices struck down a local liquor law, they encouraged liquor producers and merchants to think that they could shirk the burdens of political persuasion and accommodation.

The Justices repeatedly taught the temperance movement that compromise was not feasible and repeatedly taught the liquor industry that compromise was not necessary. Both factions came to accept the winner-takes-all game promoted by the Court. Those at the head of the dry ranks kept pressing their campaign into new and hostile territories, even against formidable resistance, seeking to impose their wills and their ways upon more and more people.

The interesting questions here concern the Court. Why did the Justices consider the effective enforcement of state liquor laws, and a modest decrease in the overall volume of interstate commerce, too heavy a sacrifice to make to the ideal of self-government? Why did they fear to allow their fellow citizens to set standards of behavior which varied from one region to the next? Why did they find local measures, partial measures, compromises, the work-a-day give and take of a decentralized law and politics, an unwelcome prospect? The Justices may have cared little about the liquor industry. Plainly they cared a great deal about the commercial life of the nation. But they could not have been unaware of their nation's vigorous tradition of leaving political authority, as to many important concerns, with state and local governments.

At its national convention in 1913, the Anti-Saloon League of America, for years the most visible and most effective opponent of the liquor industry, launched a campaign to make prohibition the law of the land by an amendment to the Constitution of the United States. In 1914, and again in 1916, vigorous campaign efforts by the League and allied organizations led to increases in the number of anti-liquor legislators, both at the state and national levels. The likelihood of an amendment making its way through Congress seemed to be increasing.

Still, even so late as this, it was not clear that Americans had to choose between a comprehensive laissez faire as to alcoholic beverages, or a nationwide prohibition. Neither faction had been able to carry all the many authorities and jurisdictions through which Americans governed themselves. Neither faction had been able to anathematize or delegitimize the other. The fanatics and the thugs on both sides had been mostly restrained. Large-scale civil disturbances had been avoided. No citizen was legally compelled to live within either a dry area or a wet area. In many states there were both dry and wet districts, even if the dry ones were somewhat porous, distressingly porous to those who had fought for their creation. The very successes of the temperance movement, compromised as they had been by the national courts, had begun to furnish its opponents with persuasive arguments. If majorities in numerous states, covering large regions of the Republic, had brought the policies of their local governments in line with the vehemence of their citizens' sentiments; if Congress had enacted measures which sought to make those policies enforceable; if the Supreme Court, even as it had quibbled with Senators and Representatives had not dared to defy them, then the roads away from — or toward — saloons, breweries, distilleries, appeared still open to those determined to travel them. The many institutions of American governance had repeatedly reasoned about the rights and wrongs, the good and the bad of liquor, and had returned their customary answer — that there was no one answer to such questions, that there could be no single nor final resolution to such controversies. Americans had thus far successfully resisted the siren call to uniformity, to anyone's forced orthodoxy about alcoholic beverages. Americans had refused to be limited to the simplicity of extremes and opposites. They might have continued to refuse.

Unfortunately, however, unreason was then on a rampage in the world, and Americans could not isolate themselves from its effects. Europe had been at war since 1914, and the United States' entry into the conflict in 1917 created great turbulence in American politics. Alliances had to be reevaluated, accounts had to be rebalanced. A large military force was to be raised, vast resources were to be marshalled. The President and the leaders of Congress now needed the consistent cooperation of a comfortable majority of the nation's legislators, many of whom owed their seats to the temperance movement. Meanwhile the liquor industry was divided and confused, and the brewers especially, dominated by German immigrants, had suddenly become very unpopular.

Now, amidst the distractions and urgencies of war, those Americans who had fought so long and so hard against liquor found their opportunity. By December 1917, their leaders' skillful arguing and bartering had persuaded Congress to pass a proposed constitutional amendment and send it to the states for ratification — an amendment which was surpassed by few state laws, if any, in the scope and reach of its restrictions. Retaining their focus, successfully negotiating the shifting political terrain, the advocates of a dry nation now put their proposal before the American people.

Opponents of the amendment thought they had sealed its doom when they succeeded in limiting the ratification period to seven years. Many of the amendment's supporters also had doubts. How could so many local approvals be managed in such a brief interval? To the surprise of almost all, some fifteen thousand state legislators, presumably looking toward future elections, quickly said yes. On January 16, 1919, Nebraska became the thirty-sixth state to ratify, and Amendment XVIII to the Constitution of the United States became the law of the land. All but two states, Connecticut and Rhode Island, eventually ratified. This legal change was not handed down from on high. A few key leaders drafted it and got it before the public, but their work was endorsed by the many. The temperance movement earned its triumph through excellent organization and strategy, and through the persistent efforts of many thousands in its ranks.

Congress took ten months to enact a statute implementing the new constitutional mandate, a federal code similar to the stricter of the state prohibition laws. The Volstead Act, passed over the President's veto in October 1919, was in place on January 17, 1920, the effective date of the Eighteenth Amendment.*

The national liquor law, as had most of the state laws, placed the home beyond the reach of the police absent evidence that it was being used for commerce in liquors. However, since the manufacture, sale, barter, transport, import, export, delivery, furnishing, and possession of alcoholic beverages were all prohibited, how was anyone to bring such a drink, legally, into his home?

The national liquor law, as had all the state laws, contained exceptions — industrial alcohol, medicinal liquors, sacramental liquors, beer with less than one-half-percent alcohol, vinegars, ciders — to be produced and distributed only under governmental permit. Predictably, the number of physicians' prescriptions for alcoholic preparations rose sharply. Predictably, pharmacists found they had numerous new customers. Predictably, some pastors and priests took advantage of a profitable new perquisite to their religious offices. Predictably, a new line of retail merchandising appeared, its inventory consisting of supplies and paraphernalia needed to brew beer, or to ferment grapes or other fruits, or to distill pure alcohol, on a very small scale. Predictably, beer leaving the brewery in compliance with the law often became "needle beer" through the injection of a missing ingredient.

And, just as predictably, drugstore liquors, liturgical

---

* U.S. Statutes at Large, Vol. 41 Pg. 305 (National Prohibition Act, also known as the Volstead Act)

liquors, homemade liquors, and alcohol-free beer could not satisfy the demands of millions of Americans. A black market, and a surge in crime, began immediately. Soon thousands of Volstead Act prosecutions were appearing on the dockets of the nation's courts. Over the next decade the number of such cases continued to increase, and the federal prison system had to be expanded to accommodate the swelling population of inmates. Meanwhile numerous states either failed to enact prohibitory codes in support of the federal law, or declined to fund their own enforcement efforts adequately. Congress was faced with the choice of diverting an increasing share of the nation's tax revenues into police work, or giving up the pretence of taking the constitutional mandate seriously. Pretence was exactly the stance of many a Congressman — there was a hidden bar or club inside the Capitol in Washington, D.C., maintained by a coterie of Representatives and Senators who gathered to share a drink or two. Pretence was the stance of much of official America. But the federal prohibition bureau was funded and the war on drink was waged.

The results were tragic. The law was unenforceable. The demand for alcoholic beverages was simply too great, and supplying that demand too profitable, for many Americans to resist. Clandestine saloons, parlors, and clubs proliferated. Buildings were modified to contain secret rooms, and hidden doors and passageways. Many distillers and brewers continued to operate, sometimes at an obscure site, sometimes behind the façade of a lawful business. Stills went into operation in the outlying areas of large cities, sending a steady stream of moonshine to the thirsty urban populations. Across thousands of miles of coastlines and borders liquors entered the country: by railroad, by truck or automobile, by boat, even by airplane, a method of transport then quite new. Travelers came up with ingenious ways to conceal beverages in their luggage or on their persons. Some people set up bars in their homes and began selling drinks to visitors, blurring the line between friendship and commerce. Many normally law-abiding citizens became smugglers. Some of these, from ordinary stations, became suddenly wealthy. Although only a small percentage of violators were arrested and charged, the numbers threatened to overwhelm the resources of police, prosecutors, courts, and prisons. Plea bargaining and light sentences frequently were used to clear the dockets.

Gangs immediately began to assert territorial control over the handling of the highly prized contraband. New organizations seeking the huge but illegal profits became large-scale diversified criminal enterprises. Competition between these groups escalated, distressingly often, into violence. Bribery of police and other officials became common. The prospect of enforcing such a widely despised law made the prohibition bureau an unattractive employer, and the harsh methods sometimes employed by its officers provoked a dismaying amount of resistance. Some agents, but many more suspects, died. A scandalous spectacle — officers of the national government indicted by state grand juries for crimes committed in the course of their efforts to enforce federal law — was occasionally seen.

To reckon up the problems caused by the Eighteenth Amendment only in legal terms, however, is to leave the audit incomplete. Prohibition also damaged the health of many Americans. Often the liquors produced by amateurs were noxious in greater or lesser degree. On the commercial scale, the least scrupulous class of liquor vendors, now entirely outside the law, peddled liquors so foul that they would have been unsaleable in a normal market. The production of large volumes of industrial alcohol necessarily continued, and though this was denatured alcohol — mixed with various additives which rendered it repellent to the taste and unfit for consumption — the diversion of some of it to the black market could not be prevented. There were ways of cleansing that alcohol, more or less, of the additives; but, needless to say, many of those who would use such an ingredient were not too particular about the "de-denaturing." The poorest Americans were most at risk; many thousands suffered severe injury, sometimes even death, from bootleg beverages of real toxicity.

And there was a moral cost to be reckoned also. Contempt for the liquor law, circumvention of the liquor law, cynicism — these actions and attitudes became so common in the United States, during the 1920s, as to taint the era indelibly.

The error was general. The American people had succumbed to a fervent but ill-advised enthusiasm. The temperance movement had misunderstood its mission and misjudged its fellow citizens. The liquor industry had done no better; its adamant refusal to surrender any of its markets had helped provoke a reaction which closed all its markets. The political classes of the United States, most of whom probably knew better, whose best and brightest surely knew better, whose special responsibility and calling it was to know better, had failed the nation. The Justices of the Supreme Court, in particular, had taken it upon themselves to make and to maintain a divisive and polarizing change in an important law.

By the early 1930s the political environment had altered dramatically. A paralyzing economic depression had arrived, pushing the fight over liquor into the background of public affairs. The follies, the failures, the outrages of strict prohibition had changed many minds. Far from being resolved, the problems caused by liquor were being reconsidered. Several state legislatures were pre-paring special constitutional conventions to be focused upon the Eighteenth Amendment. This time Congress leapt ahead. The platform of the Democratic Party in the 1932 elections called for repeal, and when the Democrats were swept into power, Congressmen quickly drafted another constitutional amendment and sent it to the states. The new provision did not explicitly declare liquor policy a local responsibility; it did so implicitly, however, by eliminating the prohibition of the Eighteenth Amendment, and by declaring what neither Congress nor the Court had managed to utter for three decades: that the transportation into any state of liquors illegal therein was prohibited.

Surely this is one of American history's choicer ironies. The proposed amendment was what the temperance movement had been so close to winning twenty years earlier, before succumbing to its radical wing and embarking upon the ill-starred quest for a national liquor code.

In December 1933 the thirty-sixth state ratified the Twenty-First Amendment, and American states and municipalities took up again the tasks and the challenges of liquor policy. There would continue to be localities throughout the nation where alcoholic beverages could not legally be sold. There would be ongoing changes, as various communities experimented with different tax and regulatory measures. But the great struggle over liquor, if not ended, entered a long quiescent phase. A truce had been declared. Americans had reminded themselves, at the cost of much turmoil and bitterness and suffering, of a master principle which had guided the work of their founding statesmen — the principle that as to many important topics, the central government of the United States best served its citizens by doing nothing or by supporting what local governments chose to do.

The evils which the liquor reformers fought were real enough. Many lives were wasted and cut short through the abuse of strong drink. Too often the wages needed by a working family for necessities enriched the makers and sellers of liquor. Many saloons, in many American towns and cities of the time, were noisome and corrupting places, often scenes of drunken rowdiness and bases of operations for criminals and prostitutes. Thoughtful people were naturally concerned about such a blight. Responsible officials had compelling reasons to take action. But what action?

Evidently not the action taken in 1919 and repented in 1933. That action had created more problems than it solved. The cure had been worse than the disease, said Americans. Locked into intractable opposition on one issue, they found a much larger issue on which they could agree. American friends and American foes of liquor came to agree that they did not have to agree. A majority concluded that uniformity, the call to conformity and orthodoxy, the single obligatory rule for all, was here quite out of place; that here, there should be no one way; rather there would be many ways.

POSTSCRIPT

The reader may well have wondered about a case which is conspicuous by its omission here: the Dred Scott decision of 1857. Why have I taken the Supreme Court to task over Mormon polygamy but said nothing about the Court's role in the great struggle over slavery?

I do not wish to seem presumptuous nor to complicate my task with unnecessary reflections upon matters which remain current topics, very sensitive topics, to the present day. Any student of American history will be able to recite the main events leading up to the Civil War, the Dred Scott ruling being a prominent one. He or she will have interpretations to hand, and will already have learned something about the religious significance of racial conflict. A careful student will be aware of the important and even leading roles that American religious organizations played in the cause of emancipation; and of the schisms among them, threatened and actual, as hostilities approached. Nor will the thoughtful student be surprised by the theological reflections offered by Lincoln in his second inaugural address.

Here I would only point out that the great temptation for Supreme Court Justices, the opportunities afforded them to assert ultimate authority over fundamentally contested terms of the American experiment, seduced them flagrantly four years before the war. If the Court, once peace was restored, then shied away from overtly religious controversies for eight decades or so, this can perhaps be explained by the trauma which followed upon their first and most dramatic failure to do so.

Trauma haunts the minds of those involved for a long time. Sooner or later, however, memories fade, and a later generation may be tempted to dare again the bold deeds which brought their unfortunate forebears to grief. This is an old story. Probably, human nature being what it is, it is a perennial story.

In 1876, at the Centennial Exhibition in Philadelphia, Pennsylvania, a small avant-garde, a group of Americans who thought of themselves as new characters in the world — as secularists — came together. Their common purpose was the attainment of a comprehensive separation between churches and political authorities, and more generally between religion and politics, at all levels of American governance: local, state, and national. To that end they created a new organization, the National Liberal League, the purpose of which was to promote a constitutional amendment; and they drafted the amendment they desired, intending that it replace the existing First Amendment to the nation's Constitution.*

The National Liberal League's proposed new First Amendment read as follows:

> Section 1. Neither Congress nor any State shall make any law respecting an establishment of religion, or favoring any particular form of re-

---

* Phillip Hamburger, in *Separation of Church and State* (2002), Chapter 11, recounts these events. For the text of the proposed amendment see pages 299-300.

ligion, or prohibiting the free exercise thereof; or permitting in any degree a union of church and State, or granting any special privilege, immunity, or advantage to any sect or religious body or to any number of sects or religious bodies; or taxing the people of any State, either directly or indirectly, for the support of any sect or religious body or of any number of sects or religious bodies; or abridging the freedom of speech or of the press, or the right of the people peaceably to assemble and to petition the government for a redress of grievances.

Section 2. No religious test shall ever be required as a condition of suffrage, or as a qualification to any office or public trust, in any State. No person shall ever in any State be deprived of any of his or her rights, privileges, or capacities, or disqualified for the performance of any public or private duty, or rendered incompetent to give evidence in any court of law or equity, in consequence of any opinions he or she may hold on the subject of religion. No person shall ever in any State be required by law to contribute directly or indirectly to the support of any religious society or body of which he or she is not a voluntary member.

Section 3. Neither the United States, nor any State, Territory, municipality, or any civil division of any State or Territory, shall levy any tax, or make any gift, grant or appropriation, for the support, or in aid of any church, religious sect, or denomination, or any school, seminary, or institution of learning, in which the faith or doctrines of any religious order or sect shall be taught or inculcated, or in which religious practices shall be observed; or for the support, or in aid, of any religious charity or purpose of any sect, order, or denomination whatsoever.

Section 4. Congress shall have power to enforce the various provisions of this Article by appropriate legislation.

It was very wordy, compared with the First Amendment authored by the nation's founding statesmen eighty-five years earlier:

Congress shall make no law respecting an establishment of religion, or prohibiting the free exercise thereof; or abridging the freedom of speech, or of the press, or the right of the people peaceably to assemble, and to petition the Government for a redress of grievances.

But besides the contrast of verbosity and concision, there was another quite conspicuous difference.

The word "state" — which does not appear in the founders' version — is used in the National Liberal League's revised first amendment eight times. The League sought, that is, to terminate the authority of state governments as to religious concerns, an authority deliberately left with those governments in 1787 and 1791. State policies and state legislation thought to be inspired by churches or other religious organizations, or to be for their benefit, aroused the special ire and focused the reforming energies of the League's members.

A few of those members may have thought the terms of their new first amendment not only an improvement upon the original, but even perhaps a plausible inference from it. Maybe. But it is very telling that they assumed the necessity of making what was arguably implicit, quite formal and explicit. It appears that few if any Americans in 1876, even those very hostile to the influence or participation of religious associations in public affairs, were ready to argue that anything occurring since the founding era had altered the nation's religious settlement, or given the nation's government, the central government, any expanded authority over religious life.

The National Liberal League's life as an organization was short. Many of its members found that they could not agree as to what a proper secularism entailed. Many of their fellow citizens, too, had other ideas about what the Constitution meant, or should mean. The text of the First Amendment stood, and has continued to stand, as the American founders originally wrote it.

But the League's idea and purpose lived on. It is quite interesting, and at first glance surprising, that eventually, in the twentieth century, a consensus arose, at least among lawyers and judges, that the League's proposed first amendment, second edition, would have been superfluous! Today, in other words, among almost all those who take a professional interest in these concerns, the religious prohibitions originally directed only to Congress are taken to be binding upon each state government as well.

How did this come about? Why?

Amending the Constitution in the way that Article V prescribes is generally a long and arduous process:

> The Congress, whenever two thirds of both Houses shall deem it necessary, shall propose Amendments to this Constitution, or, on the Application of the Legislatures of two thirds of the several States, shall call a Convention for proposing Amendments, which, in either case, shall be valid to all Intents and Purposes, as part of this Constitution, when ratified by the Legislatures

of three fourths of the several States, or by Conventions in three fourths thereof, as the one or
the other Mode of Ratification may be proposed
by the Congress; ...

Article V requires the involvement and approval of
many thousands of local legislators; and thus, beyond
them, many millions of citizens. The political obstacles
are substantial, and were intended to be so. Efficiency, if
that is the goal, requires some means of circumventing
the difficult requirements of Article V. Convenience, at
least the convenience of a few rather than of the many,
is much better served if those few persons can change
important elements of the nation's fundamental law if
and when they think change is needed.

And indeed, as the persevering reader has seen, effica-
cious means of circumvention have been found.